AN ORKNEY FEAST

A collection of Orkney recipes

prepared and presented by Alan Bichan

Photography by Ian Cooper

Printed and Published in 2000; reprinted in 2003 by

The Orcadian Limited,
Hell's Half Acre,
Hatston,
Kirkwall,
Orkney,
KW15 1DW

ISBN 1 902957 19-9

For all who have
ever shared
our table

Acknowledgements

I am indebted to the following people, whose help was invaluable in the production of this book:

Thora Bain
Elma Bews
Kate Bichan
Maimie Bichan
Peter Bichan
Wilma Bichan
Gina and Adrian Breck
Sheila Cameron
Alan Craigie
Margaret Craigie
Mark Crook
Wilma Currie
Graham Davidson
Isabel Dennison
John Devine
Jessie Drever
Margaret Drever
Olive Drever
Millie Duncan
Roger Finn
Isla and Roy Flett
Ruby Foubister
Judith Glue
Ray and Dorothy Gould
Alan Gray
James Harcus
Bena Hogan
Harvey Johnston
Jolly's Fishmonger
Allan and Vivia Leslie
John Leslie

Lobban's Butcher
Dod McConnachie
Lesley Mackay
David and Margo MacPherson
Leslie Manson
Lilias Mathers
Valerie McLellan
Christine Miller
Maureen Mowat
Elizabeth Murray
Joanna Nelson
Eddie and Anne Nicolson
Orkney Seafayre
Charlie and Muriel Rendall
Katherine and George Rendall
Stewart Ritchie
Angela Rosie
Spencer and Erica Rosie
Norman Rushbrook
Sandra and Ian Rushbrook
Malcolm Russell
Jim Scott
Audrey and Richard Shearer
Carol Sunter
Malcolm Sutherland
Marie and Eoin Sutherland
Alton Tait
Grace and Leslie Tait
Marion Tait
Sara Tait
Bessie Thomson

Introduction

Orkney is a paradise for food and drink. Only when you consider the long list of Orcadian products, do you begin to realise what an abundant larder we have in our islands. Seafood, meat, vegetables, fruit, dairy produce, whisky and beer are just some of the ingredients in our sumptuous store.

However, it is not merely the multiplicity of products that makes Orkney food so special, it is also the supreme quality of that produce which, in many cases, is unrivalled anywhere in the world.

The recipes in this book are inspired by this richness of raw produce. Some of them are traditionally Orcadian, such as clapshot and bere bannocks, whilst others, although more exotic, are based primarily on Orkney ingredients.

I have also tried to present recipes of varying complexity. Some are quick and easy, whilst others are time consuming and elaborate. This way there should be something for everyone.

As I have compiled these recipes, I have become increasingly amazed that they are based on the yield of only a small group of islands, which battle against the elements for much of the year. I hope that this book is, in some small measure, a reflection of that rich harvest.

Alan Bichan

Notes on Recipes

OVEN TEMPERATURES AND COOKING TIMES
These are approximate and should be adapted to suit individual appliances.

METRIC AND IMPERIAL
Follow the instructions for one set of measurements only.

INGREDIENTS
Wherever possible, use fresh Orkney produce.

EGGS
Use free-range eggs. These should be medium or large, unless specifically stated.

PEPPER
Black or white pepper may be used at the discretion of the reader, unless specifically stated.

Contents

Soups and Starters   13

Fish   29

Eggs and Cheese   49

Vegetables   59

Meat   79

Desserts   103

Bakes   121

Drinks   137

Soups and Starters

Enter any Orkney farmhouse in bygone days and you would frequently find a pot of broth simmering over a peat fire or on the hob. Soups have been part of our staple diet for many years.

Nowadays, we have such a range of seafood, vegetables and so on, lending themselves to soups and starters, that we are spoilt for choice. Local restaurants exploit these delicacies to the full and give us some of the most appealing first courses imaginable. The following pages include a few of my own favourites.

Thorgils said, "All that worries me now is this: suppose I come into a house and find a cup of ale, a bowl of broth, and a woman, which shall I take first?"

"Take the broth before it cools," said Thorgrim.

Men of Ness, Eric Linklater

13

Tattie Soup

(serves 8)

This easy soup is my great-grandmother's recipe. Best made using old potatoes, it is amazingly flavoursome, with beef dripping substituting for stock.

2 lb (900g) potatoes, peeled and chopped

2 pints (1 litre 200ml) water

2 medium onions, chopped

5 oz (150g) beef dripping

salt and pepper

1 Place all the ingredients in a saucepan. Bring to the boil, cover and simmer for 30 minutes.

2 Then remove from the heat and mash the potatoes. Adjust the seasoning and serve with oatcakes.

Easy Garden Turnip Soup

(serves 4-6)

If you have a glut of summer turnips, you'll find the following recipe a sweet and delicate solution.

1¾ lb (800g) garden turnips, peeled and diced

1 large onion, chopped

1½ pints (900ml) vegetable or chicken stock

salt and pepper

onion tops, cut into rings

1 Simply place the turnips and onions into a saucepan. Pour over the stock and season well.

2 Cover and cook for 30 minutes. Whizz with an electric mixer until smooth and serve with the onion rings as a garnish.

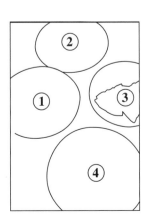

KEY

1   Beetroot Soup – *Page 19*

2   Cream of Mussel Soup – *Page 18*

3   Oatcakes – *Page 129*

4   Tattie Soup – *Page 15*

Consommé of Swede with Highland Park Whisky and Fresh Sage

(serves 6)

This is, without doubt, a time consuming recipe, but one which will make a special opening to any dinner party. Do not be tempted to cut corners with the stock or the end result will not be so good.

For the stock

2 lb (900g) lamb bones, (or beef, if available), browned for 40 minutes in the oven

8 oz (225g) mixed vegetables, chopped (e.g. carrots, celery, onion, leeks)

2 tomatoes, chopped

bouquet garni (bay leaf, thyme, parsley)

10 peppercorns

4 pints (2 litres 400ml) cold water

For the consommé

3 pints (1 litre 800ml) of the stock

2 lb (900g) swede, diced

1 tbsp tomato purée

2 egg whites

2 tbsp Highland Park whisky

salt and white pepper

fresh sage leaves

1 To make the stock, place the pre-browned bones over the vegetables, tomatoes and herbs in a large pot. Add the peppercorns and cover with the water.

2 Now bring to simmering point, skim the surface and cover. Allow to simmer for 3 hours, skimming frequently and adding a little more water if the stock reduces. Strain immediately.

3 For the consommé, cook the swede and tomato purée in the stock for 40 minutes.

4 Then strain through muslin, squeezing out as much moisture as possible. Discard the swede and allow the liquid to cool.

5 Next, using a whisk and a clean saucepan, beat the liquid into the egg whites. Place the soup on a very low heat, bring to simmering point and cook slowly, uncovered, for 40 minutes. Do **not** allow to boil, otherwise the soup will remain cloudy.

6 Lastly pour the liquid through layers of muslin. Return to the heat, add the whisky and season. Serve in bowls with 3-4 herb leaves floating on top. A slightly sweet bread such as sultana loaf goes well with this.

Pea and Potato Soup

(serves 4-6)

Fresh peas create a lighter flavour and texture than the dried peas of hearty
winter soups, making this an ideal soup for summer.

2 oz (50g) butter

1 large onion, chopped

1 lb (450g) new potatoes, scrubbed and diced

1½ pints (900ml) vegetable or chicken stock

8 oz (225g) fresh or frozen peas

2 tbsp chopped, fresh mint (or 2 tsp dried)

salt and pepper

single cream or natural yoghurt

1 First melt the butter in a saucepan and soften the onion and potatoes for a few minutes. Add the stock, peas, mint and seasoning.

2 Then bring to simmering point, cover and cook for 30 minutes.

3 Purée in a blender or rub through a sieve. Reheat and serve in bowls with a swirl of cream or yoghurt.

Broccoli and Lemon Soup

(serves 6-8)

This light soup makes a good start to a large meal. I think it is especially suitable for
Christmas Day.

1½ oz (35g) butter

1 large onion, chopped

2 large potatoes, peeled and diced

1 lb (450g) broccoli, washed, trimmed
  and roughly chopped

1¾ pints (1 litre) chicken or vegetable stock

juice and grated rind of one lemon

salt and pepper

5 fl oz (150ml) single cream

1 Melt the butter in a pot and soften the onion and potatoes for about 5 minutes.

2 Then add the broccoli, stock, lemon juice, lemon rind and seasoning. Cover and cook for 20 minutes.

3 Strain the soup and put the vegetables, together with a little of the liquid, into a food processor. Whizz until smooth.

4 Return this mixture to the liquid and stir.

5 Reheat gently with the cream and serve.

Cream of Mussel Soup

(serves 6)

Fresh Orkney mussels are the basis of this rich soup which is guaranteed to satisfy
any shellfish lover's palate.

1½ oz (35g) butter
1 large onion, chopped
2 garlic gloves, finely chopped
2 lb (900g) mussels
7 fl oz (200ml) dry white wine
12 fl oz (350ml) water
4 medium potatoes, peeled and chopped

freshly ground black pepper
1-2 tbsp brandy
5 fl oz (150ml) single cream
salt

For the garnish

6 small mussels
4 tbsp dry white wine

1 Melt the butter in a large saucepan and sweat the onion until soft, adding the garlic towards the end of the cooking time.

2 Meanwhile, scrub the mussels in fresh water and remove their beards. Discard any that are open.

3 Next pour the wine over the onions and add the mussels. Cover the saucepan and cook until the mussels open, shaking the pan occasionally. Cooking times vary from 4 to 7 minutes, depending on the size of the shells.

4 Now, using a slotted spoon, remove the mussels to a large bowl. Add the water and potatoes to the saucepan. Season well with black pepper, cover and simmer until the potatoes are soft.

5 Meanwhile, remove the mussels from their shells, discarding any that have refused to open. Reserve any juice and onions which adhere to the shells.

6 When the potatoes are cooked, liquidise the contents of the saucepan along with the mussels and their juice. For perfect results, the soup now needs to be passed through a sieve to ensure absolute smoothness of texture.

7 Reheat gently, adding the brandy, cream and a little salt.

8 For the garnish, clean the six small mussels and, using a covered saucepan, cook them in the wine until the shells open. Serve the soup in bowls with a mussel shell in each.

Beetroot Soup

(serves 8-10)

Of Russian origin, this soup is well suited to Orkney. All the vegetables in the soup grow locally and the high starch content helps fight off the winter cold. In addition, it has a sublimely rich colour, which provides a feeling of welcome in any meal.

2 medium large onions, sliced	*1 large potato, peeled and grated*
2 oz (50g) butter	*2 bay leaves*
2 cloves garlic, finely chopped	*1 tsp dried thyme*
3 pints (1 litre 800ml) good beef stock	*2 tsp sugar*
1 lb 4 oz (560g) beetroot, uncooked, peeled and diced	*salt and black pepper*
	2 tbsp lemon juice
1 lb (450g) swede, peeled and diced	*5 fl oz (150ml) soured cream or natural yoghurt*

1 Using a large pot, sweat the onions in the butter until soft, adding the garlic for the last minute or two.

2 Then pour over the stock and add all the vegetables, herbs, sugar and seasoning. Bring to the boil and simmer, covered, for one hour or until the beetroot is cooked.

3 Stir in the lemon juice, remove the bay leaves and check the seasoning.

4 Serve in bowls, each with a spoon of soured cream or yoghurt.

Deep Fried Scallops in Quick Marie Rose Sauce

(serves 4)

This makes an interesting alternative to prawn cocktail. The quick Marie Rose sauce uses salad cream in place of fresh cream, which means all the ingredients can be found in your store cupboard.

4 tbsp salad cream	*5 fl oz (150ml) water*
4 tbsp tomato ketchup	*1 tbsp oil*
1½ tbsp lemon juice	*1 small egg white, whisked until stiff*
3 tsp Worcestershire sauce	*8 medium large scallops, removed from their shells, inedible parts discarded, washed and patted dry*
2 oz (50g) cornflour	
2 oz (50g) plain flour	*oil for frying*
1 tsp baking powder	*salad leaves of your choice*
1 level tsp salt	*lemon slices*

1 To make the sauce, simply stir together the first 4 ingredients.

2 Then make the batter by sifting the flours, baking powder and salt into a bowl. Gradually mix in the water and whisk until smooth. Next add the oil and fold in the egg white.

3 Now cut each scallop into three and coat the pieces in the batter. Deep fry in hot oil, a few pieces at a time, for 1 to 2 minutes only.

4 Serve immediately on plates with the sauce, salad and lemon slices.

Sweet Cured Herring
with Pasta and Grapes

(serves 4)

Considering the diversity of ingredients here, it is amazing that the end product has such a well-rounded flavour. Try to use grapes which are not too sweet, to counterbalance the oiliness of the fish.

1 tub (500g) sweet cured herring
1½ oz (35g) short cut spaghetti
1 medium onion, sliced and separated into rings
2 tbsp oil

1 rounded tsp Cajun seasoning
2 tbsp natural yoghurt
4 oz (110g) green grapes, halved and deseeded
snipped chives (to garnish)

1 Strain the herring (reserving the marinade) and cut into thin strips.

2 Then boil the spaghetti until 'al dente' (see packet instructions). Strain and refresh in cold water. Pat dry with a towel.

3 Sauté the onion in the oil along with the Cajun seasoning until just tender. Remove from the heat and allow to cool before stirring in the yoghurt and 2 tablespoons of the marinade.

4 Now mix the herring, spaghetti, yoghurt mixture and grapes carefully in a bowl.

5 Divide the mixture between 4 plates, garnish with the chives and serve with fairy toast.

Marinated Fried Haddock

(serves 4)

This certainly gets the taste buds going. Best made a day in advance, it is eaten cold
and is good with some Orkney brown bread.

3 x 5 oz (150g) haddock fillets	1 small red pepper, pith and seeds removed, and chopped
4 tbsp olive oil	grated rind and juice of half a lemon
salt and black pepper	4 fl oz (100ml) white wine vinegar
1 medium onion, sliced	4 fl oz (100ml) water
1 clove garlic, crushed	1 oz (25g) sugar
½ inch (1 cm) piece root ginger, peeled and finely chopped	dash Worcestershire sauce

1 Cut each fish into 4 pieces and fry them in 3 tablespoons of the oil until just cooked. Remove them to a dish and season lightly.

2 Then pour the rest of the oil into the pan and soften the onion for a few minutes. Add the garlic, ginger and pepper, and cook gently for a further 2 minutes.

3 Now add all the other ingredients along with some more seasoning. Bring to the boil and simmer for 2-3 minutes without covering.

4 After that pour this mixture over the fish and allow to cool.

5 Cover the dish and chill for at least 24 hours. Allow 3 pieces of fish per person when serving.

Alan's Tip:

*"Cut onions in half before you peel them.
The skin can be removed much more easily."*

Salmon Mousse with Ginger and Orange

(serves 6-8)

Try serving this with some crisp fairy toast for an appealing starter. Alternatively, you might like to include the mousse next time you make a buffet meal.

For the stock

17 fl oz (500ml) water
5 fl oz (150ml) dry white wine
1 medium onion, chopped
1 medium carrot, chopped
8 peppercorns
1 bay leaf
a few parsley stalks
salt
2 tbsp lemon juice

For the mousse

1 lb (450g) salmon, bone in
2 heaped tsp chopped root ginger
grated rind of 1 orange
10 fl oz (300ml) double cream
4 oz (110g) cucumber
2 tbsp natural yoghurt
salt and pepper
½ oz (11g sachet) powdered gelatine
cucumber slices, to garnish

1 Put all the stock ingredients into a saucepan and simmer, covered, for 15 minutes. Strain and discard the vegetables.

2 Place the salmon, ginger and orange rind in a saucepan. Pour over the stock, cover and poach until cooked (about 8-10 minutes). Remove from the heat and allow to cool slightly.

3 Meanwhile, lightly whip the cream in a food processor. Add the cucumber, yoghurt and seasoning but do not process until other ingredients are ready.

4 Remove the salmon from the stock, discard the skin and bones, and add the flesh to the food processor. Strain the stock, reserving the orange rind and ginger to add to the salmon and other ingredients.

5 Next measure 5 fl oz (150ml) of the stock into a small bowl and sprinkle over the gelatine. Place the bowl over a saucepan of gently simmering water and stir until dissolved. Allow to cool a little before pouring this, too, into the processor.

6 Whizz until smooth, adjust the seasoning and pour into an oiled 1½ pint (900ml) mould or 6 to 8 ramekins. Chill for a few hours.

7 Finally turn out the mousse and garnish with cucumber slices.

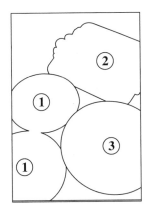

KEY
1   Stuffed Baked Tomatoes – *Page 27*
2   Salmon Mousse with Ginger and Orange – *Page 23*
3   Fried Orkney Cheese with Rhubarb Vinaigrette
      and Soured Cream – *Page 25*

Salmon Fishcakes with Madeira and Mushrooms

(serves 6)

You can simplify this recipe by serving the fishcakes with some dressed lettuce leaves. Should you try the complete recipe, however, you'll find the flavours exquisite. Use sherry in place of Madeira, if you want to cut costs.

11 oz (300g) piece of salmon, bone in

half a small onion, finely chopped

water

12 oz (340g) cooked potatoes, mashed

1 egg white

salt and pepper

1 tbsp chopped parsley

plain flour

1 egg and 1 egg yolk, lightly beaten

breadcrumbs, made from 2 large slices, thoroughly dried bread

3 fl oz (75ml) Madeira (or sherry)

7 oz (200g) button mushrooms, sliced

oil for frying

6 oz (175g) butter, cubed and chilled

extra parsley, for a garnish

1 Place the salmon in a saucepan, add the onion and merely cover with water. Simmer gently for a few minutes until just cooked. Remove the fish to a plate and allow to cool. Strain the stock and reserve.

2 Then skin the salmon, remove the bones and flake the flesh into a bowl. Add the potatoes, egg white, seasoning and 1 tablespoon of parsley. Mix well.

3 Now divide the mixture into 18 portions and, using wet hands, form each into a ball. Dip them first into flour, then egg and finally breadcrumbs. Chill until required.

4 Pour the stock into a saucepan. Add the Madeira along with the mushrooms and cook for 2 minutes. Remove the mushrooms and keep them warm. Then reduce the liquid until only 6 fluid ounces (175ml) remain.

5 Deep or shallow fry the fishcakes in the oil until crisp and heated through.

6 Meanwhile, remove the stock from the heat and gradually whisk in the butter. A hand held electric whisk is best for this. Then return the mushrooms to the sauce, season and warm gently.

7 To serve, divide the sauce between 6 heated plates and place 3 fishcakes on top of each. Garnish with parsley.

Fried Orkney Cheese with Rhubarb Vinaigrette and Soured Cream

(serves 4)

You can serve these fried cheese slices with a simple salad, but a sharp rhubarb vinaigrette along with some soured cream make more interesting accompaniments. If you shallow fry the cheese slices, rather than deep fry in cubes, you will achieve perfect results more easily.

8 oz (225g) Orkney farm cheese (not too crumbly) cut into quarter inch slices	*1 tbsp water*
1 egg, beaten	*1 tbsp white wine vinegar*
white breadcrumbs, made from dried bread slices	*1 tbsp sherry*
oil	*5 fl oz (150ml) soured cream*
8 oz (225g) rhubarb, washed and chopped	*a few snipped chives*
1 tbsp sugar	*lemon slices*

1 First dip the cheese in the egg and then the breadcrumbs. Chill for at least an hour.

2 Meanwhile, cook the rhubarb, uncovered, with the sugar and water until soft and pulpy. Stir occasionally to prevent sticking. Add the vinegar, sherry and a little more sugar, if you want. Then mash with a potato masher.

3 In a frying pan, heat the oil until almost smoking. Fry the cheese, 3 or 4 slices at a time, for only 10 seconds each side. If you fry them too long, the cheese will leak out.

4 Arrange the slices attractively on plates, with the warm rhubarb vinaigrette and some cold soured cream. Garnish with the chives and lemon slices. Serve with bannocks to mop up the vinaigrette.

Haggis Cannelloni with a Spicy Tomato Sauce

(serves 4)

Two cultures blend here to provide this unusual and tasty starter. You can add more chilli if you like but the amount shown below caters for most tastes.

8 sheets lasagne
boiling, salted water with a splash of oil
10 oz (275g) haggis
1 tbsp top of the milk
1 tbsp whisky
1 fat clove garlic, crushed
¼ level tsp chilli powder

1 tbsp olive oil
12 fl oz (350ml) tomato juice
1 tbsp lemon juice
pinch of dried thyme
dash of Worcestershire sauce
salt and freshly ground black pepper
fresh herbs (e.g. parsley, marjoram) chopped

Preheat oven to 200°C, 180°C for Fan oven, 400°F, Gas Mark 6

1 Boil the lasagne in the salted water, a few sheets at a time, for 9 minutes. Refresh in cold water and lay out, side by side, on a towel. Pat dry.

2 In a saucepan, stir the haggis, top of the milk and whisky together over a gentle heat until soft. Allow to cool.

3 Next divide the haggis between the sheets of pasta and roll them up to form tubes. Lay these, side by side, in a greased, ovenproof dish. Choose a dish that leaves only a little space between the tubes.

4 Now make the sauce by frying the garlic and chilli powder in the oil for 1 minute. Add the tomato juice, lemon juice, thyme, Worcestershire sauce and seasoning. Bring to simmering point and cook, uncovered, for about 4 minutes.

5 Strain the sauce through a sieve to remove the garlic and allow to cool before pouring it over the cannelloni tubes.

6 Cover the dish with a lid or layer of foil and set aside until ready to cook.

7 Place in the oven for 20-25 minutes or until bubbling and heated through.

8 Allow 2 tubes per person when serving. Garnish with a sprinkling of herbs.

Stuffed Baked Tomatoes

(serves 4)

Made from Orkney tomatoes, this starter can be prepared in advance and popped in the oven just before eating. Serve with fresh flour bannocks.

8 firm, medium tomatoes	grated zest of half an orange
1 very small onion, finely chopped	chopped flesh and juice of half an orange
1 oz (25g) butter	1 heaped tbsp chopped parsley
1 small tin (185g) tuna in brine, well drained	cayenne pepper

Preheat oven to 190°C, 175°C for Fan oven, 375°F, Gas Mark 5

1 Begin by slicing a lid from each tomato and scooping out the flesh and seeds.

2 Next fry the onion in the butter until soft. Remove from the heat and add the tuna and orange ingredients. Stir in the parsley and a generous dusting of cayenne pepper until all the ingredients are evenly mixed.

3 Now, using a teaspoon, stuff the tomatoes with this mixture until slightly above the tops. Flatten the filling with a knife before replacing lids.

4 Place the tomatoes in a greased ovenproof dish and bake, uncovered, for about 12 minutes or until just tender.

Grilled Oysters

(serves 4)

Oysters are traditionally eaten raw but, if this does not appeal to you, try cooking them lightly with some soured cream. This dish can also be presented as a hors d'oeuvre where it will serve 6-8 people.

16 oysters	grated Parmesan cheese
5 fl oz (150ml) soured cream	cayenne pepper
a little lemon juice	

1 Scrub the oysters and open at the hinged end with a stiff-bladed knife. Scoop out the flesh and juice into a bowl.

2 Then arrange the bigger shell halves in a grill pan, using crumpled foil to keep them absolutely level. You will probably have room for only eight shells and so will have to keep these warm while you cook the rest.

3 Into each shell pour a teaspoonful of soured cream and splash in a little lemon juice. Top each with an oyster minus the juice. If there is room, add a little more cream.

4 Sprinkle over some Parmesan cheese and grill for 4-5 minutes under a high heat.

5 Add a pinch of cayenne to each oyster and serve with crusty, brown bread.

Fish

It is impossible to be any great distance from the coast in Orkney, so it is little wonder that Orcadians have the sea in their blood and that fishing is part of our heritage.

A large range of fish species exists in the sea around Orkney. Whichever you choose to eat, however, whether it be cuithes (half grown saithe) caught on a calm summer's evening and fried for supper, haddock in batter from one of the local fish and chip shops, or poached salmon steaks from an Orkney fish farm, all will commonly have a scintillating freshness.

Shellfish also abound in our cool, clear waters. Many Orcadians enjoy a trip to gather cockles or spoots (razor clams) in springtime. Creeling for partans (crabs) and lobsters is an important industry and mussels, scallops and oysters are amongst the other shellfish which are plentiful and of excellent quality.

Anglers come from far to enjoy freshwater fishing in our beautiful lochs. Orkney brown trout are second to none, frequently having lucent, healthy skin, a firm texture and deep pink flesh. Grilled, freshly caught trout must rank as one of the most delicate and delightful tastes our county has to offer.

He straightens himself, again grasps the fishing wand and patiently renews his casting. Not without result – for a single sillock or two, attracted by this miraculous shower of food follows the flies tentatively.

Orkney Shore - Robert Rendall

Fillet of Brown Trout
with Chive Butter Sauce
(serves 4)

This is one of my all time favourites. Try serving the fish with some glazed, baby vegetables and you'll produce one of the best dishes Orkney has to offer.

For the trout

2 brown trout, each approximately 2 lb (900g) or 4 trout, each approximately 1 lb (450g)
salt and freshly milled white pepper
a little oil or butter

For the sauce

bones from the trout
4 fl oz (100ml) dry white wine
4 fl oz (100ml) water
2-3 parsley stalks
1 heaped tsp cornflour
5 oz (150g) Orkney butter, cubed
1 tbsp chives, snipped
salt and freshly milled white pepper
2 extra dashes dry white wine.

1 Gut and fillet the trout, reserving the bones for the stock. Leave on the skin. Season lightly and brush the flesh side with oil or butter. Then lay the fillets, side by side, in an oiled grill pan. Do not cook yet.

2 To make the stock put the fish bones, wine, water and parsley stalks in a saucepan. Cook for 5–10 minutes.

3 Next strain the stock and reduce until 4 fl oz (100ml) remain. Thicken with the cornflour, which has first been mixed with a little water.

4 Now grill the trout, turning once. Be sure not to overcook them. A minute or so on each side will be all that is required. When cooked, remove the skin and transfer the fish to serving dishes. Keep warm.

5 While the fish is cooking, make the sauce by removing the stock from the heat and gradually whisking in the butter cubes. An electric whisk is best for this.

6 When all the butter has been worked in, add the chives, seasoning and extra wine.

7 Serve the trout with the sauce poured over.

< Brown Trout, Harray Loch

Cuithes

(serves 4)

Cuithes (half grown saithe) are best eaten 'straight from the sea'. They can be dipped in flour before frying but I find salted oatmeal gives a hot, crisp coating which is lovely with the sweet flavoured fish.

4 cuithes	salt
a little milk	3 oz (75g) butter
2 oz (50g) medium or fine oatmeal	

1 Gut the fish, removing the heads, fins and tails but leaving the bones and skin.

2 Then dip the fish in milk. Mix the oatmeal with some salt and use this to coat the skin.

3 Next melt the butter in a frying pan and, when it sizzles, add the fish. Fry for about 5-7 minutes on each side or until the flesh flakes easily.

4 Serve with bere bannocks and butter.

Fish Pie

(serves 4-5)

You can increase the smoked flavour in this dish by adding more smoked haddock and decreasing the amount of fresh fish. I find, however, equal amounts of each just perfect.

8 oz (225g) smoked haddock fillet, skinned	freshly ground black pepper
8 oz (225g) fresh haddock fillet, skinned	a little salt
3 oz (75g) butter	4 oz (110g) cooked peas
2 oz (50g) plain flour	4 tomatoes, sliced
1 pint (600ml) milk	mashed potatoes, seasoned (made from 2 lb 4 oz
3 oz (75g) Orkney Cheddar, grated	(1 kg) raw, peeled potatoes)

Preheat oven to 200°C, 180°C for Fan oven, 400°F, Gas Mark 6

1 Begin by frying the fish in the butter until just cooked. Then remove to a plate, shaking off excess butter.

2 Next transfer the butter to a saucepan and stir in the flour. Allow to cook for a few moments before stirring in the milk, a little at a time.

3 Then mix in the cheese until melted. Season generously with black pepper and add the salt and peas.

4 Now flake the fish into a flat, ovenproof dish. Pour over the sauce and cover with the tomato slices.

5 Top with the mashed potato and bake for 30-35 minutes.

Salt Haddock with Tatties and Melted Orkney Butter

(serves 4)

I've given both methods of removing excess salt from the fish in this recipe.
Whichever one you choose, I'm sure you'll agree this is simple food at its best.

4 pieces salt haddock, each about 5 oz (150g)	*4 oz (110g) Orkney butter*
potatoes, peeled (enough for 4)	*chopped parsley (optional)*

METHOD 1

1 Soak the haddock for at least 8 hours in a large bowl of cold water. If you change the water once or twice during this time, you will further reduce the salt level, which might be more to your taste.

2 Boil the potatoes without salt until tender. Strain and dry thoroughly.

3 Meanwhile, put the fish into a pot, cover with plenty of cold water and boil for 10 minutes. Then strain.

4 Melt the butter and serve with the fish and potatoes. Garnish with the chopped parsley, if used.

METHOD 2

1 Place the fish in a fairly large saucepan and cover with cold water.

2 Bring to near boiling point. Then discard the water. As in the previous method, if you repeat this process once or twice, you will extract more salt from the fish.

3 Continue as for Method 1.

Baked Haddock with Cous Cous and Roast Vegetable Stuffing

(serves 4)

Fresh Orkney haddock here meets a filling of Mediterranean character that is full of colour, flavour and texture.

2 fresh haddock, cleaned but with heads still on, each weighing about 1½ lb (675g)
olive oil
1 medium courgette, chunked
1 small red pepper, deseeded, pith removed and roughly chopped

1 fat clove garlic, chopped
salt and freshly ground black pepper
4 fl oz (120ml) water
4 oz (110g) cous cous
1½ oz (35g) butter

Preheat oven to 200°C, 180°C for Fan oven, 400°F, Gas Mark 6

1 Remove the fish heads and, using a sharp knife, extend the body cavity to the tail. Set aside.

2 Next grease a roasting tin with olive oil. Place the courgette, pepper and garlic on the tin, season generously and drizzle with some more olive oil. Bake for 15 minutes.

3 Allow the vegetables to cool. Then put them on a chopping board, being careful to add all the olive oil and garlic from the roasting tin. Chop finely using a large knife.

4 Bring the water to the boil in a small saucepan. Add the cous cous, cover and allow to stand for 3 minutes without returning to the heat. Season lightly and stir in the butter until absorbed. Allow to cool.

5 Now mix the vegetables with the cous cous and use to stuff the two fish. Place the haddock side by side on a greased roasting tin (the one you used for the vegetables is ideal). Drizzle over some olive oil and set aside until ready to cook.

6 Bake the fish for 20-25 minutes in an oven preheated to 190°C, 170°C for Fan oven, 375°F, Gas Mark 5. Allow half a fish each when serving.

Smoked Haddock Pasty with Lemon and Caper Sauce

(serves 4)

This recipe makes 4 generous helpings and, served with the sauce, the pasties need no other accompaniment.

For the pasty

12 oz (340g) smoked haddock fillet
2 oz (50g) butter
2 shallots, chopped
1 small red pepper, chopped
1 tomato, peeled and chopped
1 egg and 1 egg yolk
salt and black pepper
2 tbsp parsley, finely chopped
2 tbsp fresh breadcrumbs
12 oz (340g packet) puff pastry, thawed if frozen
1 extra egg, beaten

For the sauce

4 oz (110g) butter
2 tbsp lemon juice
1 clove garlic, crushed
2 tsp capers, finely chopped
black pepper

Preheat oven to 190°C, 175°C for Fan oven, 375°F, Gas Mark 5

1 Begin by cooking the fish in a little water until it flakes easily. Strain and remove the skin. Then break the fish into small pieces and place these in a large bowl to cool.

2 Next melt the butter and fry the shallots gently until soft.

3 Add the red pepper and tomato, cooking these for 2 minutes only. Remove from the heat and allow to cool.

4 Now stir the shallot mixture into the bowl with the fish. Add the egg, egg yolk, a little salt, black pepper, parsley and breadcrumbs to form the filling for the pasty. Mix well.

5 Roll out the pastry to make a 13 inch (32 cm) square. Cut this into quarters and divide the filling between these four smaller squares.

6 Fold each over diagonally to form a triangle. Pinch the edges, brush with the beaten egg and pierce with a knife.

7 These can now be refrigerated for up to 12 hours. When ready to cook, place them on a greased baking sheet and bake for 25-30 minutes or until the pastry is cooked and the filling thoroughly heated.

8 Meanwhile, make the sauce by melting the butter in a saucepan, adding the rest of the ingredients and cooking for 10 seconds.

9 Serve the pasty with the hot sauce.

Cod in Filo Pastry with Tarragon Cream Sauce

(serves 4)

This makes a good dinner party dish. The marinade in the recipe provides the cod with extra flavour and forms the basis for the sauce.

2 pieces cod fillet, each about 8 oz (225g)	1 pack filo pastry (12 sheets), defrosted
3 fl oz (75ml) dry white wine	melted butter
½ tbsp lemon juice	3 oz (75g) prawns, defrosted if frozen
2 tbsp olive oil	1 medium red pepper, deseeded and chopped small
1 small onion, finely chopped	1 tsp dried tarragon
salt	5 fl oz (150ml) double cream
black pepper	2 oz (50g) butter, diced and chilled

Preheat oven to 200°C, 180°C for Fan oven, 400°F, Gas Mark 6

1 Begin by cutting the fillets in half to form four roughly square pieces.

2 In a flat dish, mix the wine, lemon juice, oil, onion and seasoning. Add the fish, cover and marinate for one and a half hours, turning occasionally.

3 Carefully lay one sheet of filo on a work surface and brush with melted butter. Place another sheet on top of the first, again brushing with butter.

4 Next put a piece of cod on the pastry sheets. Season lightly and top with a quarter of the prawns, red pepper and onions, strained from the marinade.

5 Cover with a third sheet of filo, brushing with butter as before. Then fold up the edges of the pastry untidily, to form a rough parcel.

6 Now repeat this process using the remaining three pieces of fish and place all four parcels on a greased baking sheet. Bake for 30 minutes or until golden and cooked through.

7 Meanwhile, make the sauce. Put the marinade, tarragon and half the cream in a saucepan. Bring to the boil and reduce by half.

8 Remove from the heat and whisk in the butter, a piece at a time. Stir in the rest of the cream and reheat gently.

9 Serve the fish parcels with the cream sauce.

Cod Steaks with Leeks and Mushrooms

(serves 4)

Cooking your side vegetables in the sauce makes this fish dish quick and easy.
Monkfish is also good served in this manner.

4 cod steaks (or 4 pieces of cod fillet)	salt and pepper
a little flour	1 medium leek, coarse leaves removed and sliced
2 tbsp oil	6 oz (175g) button mushrooms, sliced
2 oz (50g) butter	3 fl oz (75ml) dry Vermouth

1 Coat the fish lightly in flour and fry them gently in the oil and butter until just cooked. Season lightly, remove from the pan and keep warm in a low oven.

2 Then, with the heat low, add the leek and mushrooms to the pan. Cook them for about 2 minutes, turning occasionally.

3 Pour over the Vermouth, turn up the heat and reduce by half. Season lightly.

4 Serve the cod steaks with the leek and mushroom sauce poured over.

Sole with Orange and Marjoram Sauce

(serves 2)

The sauce here is simplicity itself and can be used with any white fish.

1½ oz (35g) butter	½ level tsp sugar
2 sole fillets	pinch of marjoram
juice of 1 small orange	salt and pepper
1 tsp orange rind	

1 Begin by melting the butter in a frying pan. When it sizzles, add the sole fillets upside down and fry for about a minute.

2 Add all the other ingredients except the salt and pepper, turn the fish fillets over and allow the juices to bubble around them.

3 Cook until the fish just begin to flake. Then remove them to serving dishes.

4 Season the sauce lightly and pour it over the sole fillets.

Plaice Fillets Stuffed with Rice and Elderflowers

(serves 4)

Make this most delicate of fish dishes in July, when Orkney's elderflower trees are awash with blossoms

1 oz (25g) butter	1 tomato, skinned, deseeded and chopped
1-2 shallots, chopped	8 elderflower sprays, blossoms removed with a fork
3 oz (75g) Basmati rice, washed	salt and pepper
7 fl oz (200ml) water	4 fairly large plaice fillets, skinned
	a little white wine

Preheat oven to 200°C, 180°C for Fan oven, 400°F, Gas Mark 6

1 Melt half the butter in a saucepan, add the shallots and sweat them for a few minutes.

2 Then stir in the rice and pour over the water. Bring to the boil, cover tightly and reduce the heat. Simmer for 10 minutes, by which time the rice will have absorbed the water.

3 Next stir in the tomato and elderflower blossoms. Season lightly and set aside until cold.

4 Butter an ovenproof dish and lay out the fillets in this, one at a time, placing a quarter of the rice mixture on each one. Roll up the fillets over the stuffing, splash with a little wine and dot with the remaining butter.

5 Cover with foil and bake for 25–30 minutes or until cooked through.

6 If desired, you can cook a little extra stuffing to serve with the fish.

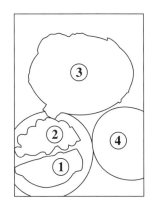

KEY
1   Fillet of Brown Trout with Chive Butter Sauce – *Page 31*
2   Glazed Baby Vegetables in Orkney Butter – *Page 73*
3   Highland Lobster – *Page 47*
4   Plaice Fillets Stuffed with Rice and Elderflowers – *Page 39*

Salmon Steaks with Yoghurt Sauce

(serves 4)

This sharp sauce is a favourite of mine with salmon. It is also a suitable accompaniment for sea trout.

9 fl oz (260ml) natural yoghurt	*1 level tsp caster sugar*
3 egg yolks	*salt and pepper*
2 heaped tsp pickled capers, chopped	*4 salmon steaks*
2 tsp caper vinegar (from the caper jar)	*a little butter*

1 Combine the yoghurt, egg yolks, capers, vinegar and sugar in a bowl until evenly mixed.

2 Then set the bowl over a saucepan of simmering water and cook for 15-20 minutes or until the sauce thickens slightly. Whisk frequently during the cooking process. Season lightly.

3 Meanwhile grill the salmon steaks on both sides, brushing with a little butter and checking that they do not become overcooked.

4 Season the steaks and serve with the sauce.

Smoked Salmon Parcels

(makes 10 approximately)

Serve these on a bed of lettuce, as part of a buffet.

4 oz (110g) smoked salmon	*1 tbsp lemon juice*
4 oz (110g) full cream cheese	*cayenne pepper, to taste*
1 stick celery, chopped very small	*lemon slices*
3 oz (75g) cooked chick peas (tinned will do)	

1 First cut the salmon into pieces approximately 2 inches by 3 inches (5cm by 7½ cm).

2 Combine all the other ingredients, except the lemon slices, in a bowl.

3 Lay out the salmon slices on a work surface and place a dessertspoonful of the cheese mixture on each. Then roll them up loosely and garnish with the lemon slices.

Arctic Char with Smitaine Sauce

(serves 2)

Locally farmed char has recently appeared on the Orkney menu. It has a delicate flavour and so should be cooked simply. I think smitaine sauce is the perfect accompaniment.

For the sauce

½ oz (12g) butter

1 medium shallot, peeled and finely diced

2 fl oz (50ml) dry white wine

4 fl oz (125ml) soured cream

salt and freshly ground black pepper

dash of lemon juice

For the fish

2 x 6 oz (175g) char fillets, skinned

salt

1½ oz (35g) butter

1 To make the sauce, melt the butter in a saucepan and cook the shallot until soft.

2 Pour in the wine and bubble until only a trace of liquid remains.

3 Now add the soured cream and simmer for 3-4 minutes. Season to taste and splash in the lemon juice. Keep warm.

4 Season the char lightly with salt and fry gently in the butter on both sides until just cooked. This will only take about 2 minutes.

5 Serve the fish with the sauce poured over.

Herring with Fried Apple and Glazed Brussels Sprouts

(serves 2)

People might look twice at the combination of ingredients in this recipe. I can assure you, however, that the flavours work well together.
You might also like to try mackerel served in this way.

2 oz (50g) butter	7-8 oz (200-225g) Brussels sprouts, outer leaves removed
2 herring fillets, coated in oatmeal	salted water
1 dessert apple, cored and sliced	1 tsp sugar

1 Melt the butter in a frying pan and fry the herring gently on both sides until cooked through. Then remove the fish and keep them warm.

2 Now fry the apple slices, turning them once and watching they do not become too soft. Remove them to a warm place.

3 While the herring and apple slices are cooking, boil the sprouts in the salted water until cooked but still crunchy. Strain off the water.

4 If the frying pan is dry, add a little more butter. When it sizzles, add the sprouts and sprinkle over the sugar. Fry for a few moments, allowing the sprouts to roll around the pan and become evenly glazed.

5 Serve the herring with the apple slices and sprouts.

Halibut Steaks with Piquant Paprika Butter

(serves 4)

I think halibut is best grilled or fried rather than cooked in liquid so that its meaty texture is preserved. This incredibly easy recipe illustrates the point.

4 x 6-7 oz (175-200g) halibut steaks	juice of one lime
salt and freshly ground black pepper	1 scant tbsp white wine vinegar
4 oz (110g) butter	lime slices (to garnish)
1 rounded tsp paprika	

1 Begin by seasoning the halibut on both sides. Then lay them, side by side, on a grill pan.

2 Melt the butter in a saucepan and allow to sizzle for a few moments. Add the paprika and cook for a few moments more. Stir in the lime juice and wine vinegar.

3 Next brush the halibut lightly with the butter mixture.

4 Grill for a few minutes under a medium heat until half cooked through.

5 Now turn the fish over and brush generously with the remaining butter. Grill until the fish flakes easily, basting frequently with butter in the bottom of the grill pan.

6 Serve the halibut with any remaining butter spooned over and garnish with the lime slices.

Alan's Tip:

"If you are planning a meal and you can afford the space, set the table the night before you entertain so you can concentrate on cooking next day."

Turbot with Prawns and Mushrooms

(serves 4)

You can substitute haddock in this recipe but I think it is best with the firm texture of turbot.

4 x 6 oz (175g) pieces of turbot fillet
5 oz (150g) butter
4 oz (110g) button mushrooms, sliced
5 spring onions, chopped

4 oz (110g) cooked prawns, defrosted if frozen
salt and freshly ground black pepper
dash of lemon juice

1 Gently fry the turbot in the butter until the flesh flakes easily. Set the fish aside and keep warm.

2 Then add the mushrooms and onions to the pan and cook for 3-4 minutes.

3 Next add the prawns and cook for a further minute.

4 Season lightly and splash in the lemon juice.

5 Serve the turbot with the contents of the pan poured over.

Cockles

(serves 4)

These are best left overnight in a bucket of fresh water to remove sand from the shells.

4½ lb (2kg) cockles, pre-soaked
vinegar (optional)

1-2 oz (25-50g) butter

1 Put the cockles in a large pot, cover and steam open the shells.

2 Divide between four plates (large soup plates are ideal) and sprinkle with vinegar if desired.

3 Alternatively remove the cockles from their shells and fry gently in the butter for a few moments.

4 Either way, serve the cockles with flour or bere bannocks.

Cockles in White Wine

(serves 4)

Normally this method of cooking is reserved for mussels, but I think it is equally well suited to cockles.

4½ lb (2kg) cockles, soaked in fresh water overnight

5 fl oz (150ml) dry white wine

1 large onion, finely chopped

2 cloves garlic, finely chopped

2 tbsp chopped parsley

1 Put all the ingredients in a large pot, cover and cook until the shells have opened.

2 Divide the cockles between four large soup plates and serve with bannocks.

Spoots

Razor fish are known as spoots in Orkney. They can be quite tricky to catch hold of, but this can be simplified by pouring a little salt into the holes they leave before attempting to grab them. The number you allow per person varies enormously. Some people may only eat 8 whilst enthusiasts may eat 20!

Spoots

butter (not margarine)

1 Place the spoots in a large pot. Cover and steam the shells open in their own juice over a high heat. Alternatively, pour boiling water over the shells and strain after they have opened.

2 Cut off and discard the inedible parts. This is very much a matter of taste, but some people eat only the fruit (smooth part) whilst others eat almost the entire spoot.

3 Heat the butter in a frying pan★ until very hot and cook the shellfish, a few at a time, for a few seconds only. They will have a tough texture if they are cooked too long.

4 Serve with bannocks.

★ Note: never try to deep-fry spoots

Partan and Avocado Mousse

(serves 10-12 approximately, as part of a buffet)

Partan (crab) meat combines well with avocados in this dish. Make it the day you intend to eat it, otherwise the mousse loses its attractive, pale green colour.

8 oz (225g) cooked crab meat	salt and pepper
1 tub (340g) cottage cheese	½ oz (11g sachet) powdered gelatine
2 avocados, peeled and stoned	4 tbsp single cream
1½ tbsp lemon juice	lemon slices (to garnish)
1 level tsp paprika	fresh herbs (to garnish)

1 Line the bottom of a 1½-1¾ pint (900-1,050ml) mould with greased greaseproof paper.

2 Put the crab, cheese, avocados, lemon juice, paprika and seasoning into a food processor and whizz until evenly amalgamated.

3 Next stir the gelatine and cream together in a cup. Bring a small saucepan of water to simmering point and place the cup in this. Stir until the gelatine has dissolved.

4 With the motor running, quickly pour the gelatine mixture through a sieve into the food processor.

5 After a few seconds, pour the contents into the mould and spread out evenly.

6 Chill for about 3 hours.

7 When ready to serve, slide a knife around the edges of the mould and turn out the mousse onto a plate. Remove the greaseproof paper and garnish with the lemon slices and herbs.

Highland Lobster

(serves 2)

For a special occasion, there is little can compare with this spectacular dish. It is unquestionably time consuming but, being made from some of the finest Orkney ingredients, it can hardly fail to impress.

1 lobster, weighing approximately 2lb (900g)	1½ oz (35g) white Orkney Cheddar, grated
1½ oz (35g) butter	1 tbsp lemon juice
1 oz (25g) button mushrooms, sliced	salt and freshly ground black pepper
2 small spring onions, chopped	1½ oz (35g) white breadcrumbs
1½ tbsp Highland Park whisky	pinch of cayenne pepper
¾ oz (18g) plain flour	a few lettuce leaves
3 fl oz (75ml) milk	parsley (to garnish)
3 fl oz (75ml) double cream	

Preheat oven to 200°C, 180°C for Fan oven, 400°F, Gas Mark 6

1 Boil the lobster for 20 minutes. Remove from the water and allow to cool.

2 Then place the lobster on its back and split it in half lengthways using a large, sharp knife.

3 Crack open the large claws and put the flesh, roughly chopped, into a bowl. Leave on the small, crawler claws.

4 Remove all lobster meat from the body cavity and chop into the bowl. Discard the sack of grit from the head and the black intestinal tube that runs down the back. Reserve any coral (found in female lobsters) and clean the shells.

5 Next melt ½ oz (12g) of the butter in a saucepan and gently fry the mushrooms and spring onions for 1-2 minutes. Pour over the whisky and set alight. When the flames have died away, set the saucepan aside to cool.

6 In another saucepan, melt the remaining butter and stir in the flour. Cook for a few moments. Then add the milk, a little at a time, stirring constantly until the sauce is smooth.

7 Now add the cream, ½ oz (12g) of the cheese, the lemon juice and seasoning, stirring over a gentle heat until the cheese has melted. Allow to cool with a layer of clingfilm on the sauce to prevent a skin forming.

8 Add the lobster flesh and the mushroom and spring onion mixture to the sauce. Sieve the coral (if used) and stir this in too. Pile the mixture into the two shells.

9 Then mix the rest of the cheese with the breadcrumbs and stir in the cayenne pepper. Spread this mixture evenly over the sauce.

10 You can now refrigerate the lobster or bake it immediately. Cook in the oven for 18-20 minutes or until the breadcrumbs are light brown. Add a few extra minutes to the cooking time if the lobster is very cold. Try not to overcook.

11 Serve on a bed of lettuce, garnished with parsley.

Eggs and Cheese

Although the golden age of Orkney's egg production is now over, many farms still keep a few hens and some even operate as a commercial venture. Free-range eggs from these farms have deeply coloured yolks and a full, fresh flavour. Duck eggs are also obtainable.

Orkney cheese divides into two main categories — factory and farm. Within these there is much variety but all types have unique characteristics which are worthy of acclaim.

Factory cheese is like Cheddar in character and comes in an assortment of colours and strengths. Prizes are frequently won in national competitions. To choose a favourite is difficult but many people relish the intensity of mature Orkney Cheddar to such an extent that they refuse to buy anything else.

Farm cheese is softer and whiter than factory varieties and can be moist, crumbly or creamy in texture. Flavoured cheese is also now available. Any one of these, when served with home-made bannocks or oatcakes and farm butter is, in truth, food of the gods.

He was aye vaigan b' the shore
An' climman amang the craigs,
Swappan the mallimaks,
Or taakan whitemaa aiggs.

Crag'sman's Widow, Robert Rendall

Scrambled Egg on Toast, '50s Style
(serves 2)

The title is, I confess, personal and nostalgic. Get all the correct ingredients and the effect is magic. Do not be tempted to add milk, however, as this dilutes the flavour.

4 free-range eggs	2½ oz (60g) butter, preferably Orkney farmhouse
salt and pepper	2 large, thick slices, cut from an unsliced plain loaf

1 Beat the eggs lightly with a fork and season now, rather than when cooked, so you can serve this up as quickly as possible.

2 Sizzle 2 oz (50g) of the butter in a saucepan. Add the eggs and cook very gently, stirring constantly. The eggs must be removed from the heat before they are completely set, so that their creamy quality is retained.

3 Stir in the remaining butter at the last minute.

4 Time things so that the toast is ready just in time. Butter lightly and spoon the scrambled eggs on top.

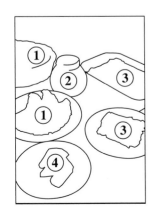

KEY
1   Pancakes Stuffed with Orkney Cheddar, Bacon and Apples – *Page 55*
2   Marinated Goat's Cheese – *Page 53*
3   Egg and Tomato Bake – *Page 54*
4   Flour Bannocks – *Page 124*

Orcadian Rarebit

(for 4 slices of toast)

Here is a version of Welsh Rarebit which includes Orkney Cheddar, free-range eggs and even a splash of home brew!

½ oz (12g) butter
4 oz (110g) coloured Orkney Cheddar, grated
pepper
dash of Worcestershire sauce

1 tbsp home brewed ale
2 small free-range eggs
4 large pieces of toast, buttered

1   Melt the butter in a saucepan and, when it sizzles, add the cheese. Stir until the cheese has melted.

2   Next season with the pepper and mix in the Worcestershire sauce and home brew.

3   Break the eggs into the saucepan and stir constantly until the mixture thickens.

4   Spoon onto the toast and serve immediately.

Grilled Cheese Omelette

(serves 2-3)

Grilling an omelette, rather than frying, produces a lighter end product.

4 free-range eggs
salt and pepper
1 tbsp cold water

2 oz (50g) butter
3 oz (75g) Orkney Cheddar, grated

1   Lightly beat the eggs with a fork. Season and stir in the water.

2   Heat a 9-10 inch (22-24 cm) frying pan and add the butter. Using a medium high heat, allow the butter to foam.

3   Pour in the eggs but do not stir as you would with an ordinary omelette. Instead, allow the base to cook whilst the top remains runny.

4   Sprinkle over the cheese and transfer the pan quickly to a very hot grill.

5   When risen and golden, serve immediately.

Marinated Goat's Cheese

Instead of a cheese board, serve up these mouth-watering slices of Orkney goat's cheese with some bannocks or oatcakes. Drizzle over some of the olive oil marinade in place of butter.

7 oz (200g) piece of goat's cheese
1 tsp green or pink peppercorns
2 cloves garlic, halved

2-3 sprigs fresh rosemary or thyme
6 fl oz (175ml) extra virgin olive oil

1 Remove the skin from the cheese and cut it into slices.

2 Then, using a perfectly clean jar, arrange the cheese slices with the peppercorns, garlic and sprigs of herb tucked between.

3 Pour over the olive oil, cover and marinate for 4-5 days.

Egg and Tomato Bake

(serves 6-8)

This is incredibly easy to make and is one of the few dishes that would suit any meal in the day, including breakfast.

6 eggs	2 fl oz (50ml) cooking oil
8 medium tomatoes, each cut into 8 pieces	1 heaped tsp dried basil
4 oz (110g) smoked sausage, chopped	salt and pepper
1 large onion, chopped	8 oz (225g) self-raising flour

Preheat oven to 190°C, 170°C for Fan oven, 375°F, Gas Mark 5

1 Beat the eggs in a large bowl. Then stir in all the other ingredients, leaving the flour to last.

2 Grease a large, flat ovenproof dish and dust the bottom and sides with flour. Add the mixture, spreading it out evenly.

3 Bake for 40 minutes or until golden and cooked through.

4 Cut into slices or squares with a sharp knife and serve immediately.

Pancakes Stuffed with Orkney Cheddar, Bacon and Apples

(serves 6)

These can be made in advance and only require a few minutes in the oven to reheat them. They are lovely for tea at any time of year, but are particularly suitable for Shrove Tuesday.

For the pancakes
3½ oz (90g) plain flour
1 pinch of salt
2 eggs, lightly beaten
8 fl oz (225ml) milk
½ tbsp oil
a little butter

For the filling
½ tbsp oil
5 oz (150g) smoked, streaky bacon, cut into pieces
3 apples, cored and cubed, but not peeled
4 oz (110g) Orkney Cheddar, grated
1 tsp English mustard
pepper

Preheat oven to 200°C, 180°C for Fan oven, 400°F, Gas Mark 6

1 To make the pancakes, begin by sifting the flour and salt into a bowl.

2 Add the eggs and gradually whisk them with the flour, pouring in a little milk if the mixture gets stiff.

3 When all the milk has been added, whisk thoroughly to remove any lumps. Then stir in the oil.

4 Next lightly grease a 10 inch (25 cm) frying pan with the butter. When it is very hot, add enough pancake batter to cover the base of the pan, tipping it from side to side as you do so.

5 Cook the pancake until light golden underneath. Then loosen the edges and flip over. When the second side is cooked, remove to a cooling wire. Repeat for the other pancakes.

6 Then make the filling. Gently heat the oil in a frying pan and cook the bacon for 3-4 minutes.

7 Now add the apples, cheese, mustard and pepper, stirring until the cheese has melted. Allow to cool.

8 Divide this mixture between 6 of the pancakes (you may have 1 or 2 extra). Then fold them in half and place them, side by side, in a large, greased ovenproof dish.

9 Bake for 10-12 minutes or until heated through.

Mayonnaise Dips with Deep Fried Potato Peelings

If you have a food processor or liquidiser, I encourage you to make your own mayonnaise. For those of you who have never done this, you'll find it easier than you think. The end result also has a much better flavour than bought varieties.

For the mayonnaise

1 large free-range egg, at room temperature
1 pinch dry mustard
1/2 tsp salt
1 tbsp white wine vinegar
9 fl oz (260ml) sunflower oil, at room temperature

For the mustard and garlic dip

1/2 above mayonnaise recipe
1 heaped tsp French mustard
1 small clove garlic, crushed
a little chopped parsley

For the tomato and prawn dip

1/2 mayonnaise recipe (left)
1 tbsp tomato sauce
1 dash Worcestershire sauce
1 dash lemon juice
1 oz (25g) cooked prawns, finely chopped
a few extra prawns

For the deep fried potato peelings

8-12 potatoes
oil

1 To make the mayonnaise, blend the egg with the mustard and salt for about 20 seconds. Then add the vinegar and blend briefly.

2 Now, with the motor running, add the oil one drop at a time to begin with. Gradually increase to a thin trickle. When all the oil is added, the mayonnaise should be very thick. Divide the mixture in two.

3 To make the mustard and garlic dip, combine the mayonnaise, mustard and garlic. Garnish with the parsley.

4 To make the tomato and prawn dip, combine all the ingredients except the whole prawns, which should be used as a garnish.

5 To make the deep fried potato peelings, begin by scrubbing the potatoes. Then peel with a sharp knife (not a potato peeler). Reserve the potatoes for another dish and keep the peelings in water until ready to fry.

6 Dry the peelings in a towel and deep fry in hot oil. When golden, serve them hot with the dips.

Kipper and Almond Soufflé

(serves 4)

You can serve this tasty dish for a light lunch. Have everyone seated at the table early as traditionally people should wait on a soufflé rather than the other way round.

1 boneless kipper, weighing 6 oz (175g)	salt and pepper
7 fl oz (200ml) milk	3 medium eggs, separated
1 oz (25g) butter	1 oz (25g) flaked almonds
1 oz (25g) plain flour	pinch of cream of tartar

Preheat oven to 200°C, 180°C for Fan oven, 400°F, Gas Mark 6

1 First put the kipper and milk into a saucepan. Bring to the boil and simmer, uncovered, for a few minutes.

2 When the flesh flakes easily, remove the fish and peel off the skin. Mash the flesh with a fork. Reserve the milk.

3 Next melt the butter in another saucepan. Add the flour and allow to cook for a few moments. Gradually stir in the milk to make a white sauce.

4 Season generously and remove from the heat. Stir in the egg yolks along with half of the flaked almonds.

5 Now whisk the egg whites with the cream of tartar until stiff. Stir 1 tablespoon of this into the sauce to slacken the mixture. Then carefully fold in the rest of the egg whites.

6 Pour the mixture into a well greased soufflé dish. A 5½ inch (14 cm) dish, with a collar tied round, is about right if you want your soufflé to rise above the edge.

7 Sprinkle with the remaining almonds and bake for 30 minutes or until risen and light brown. Serve immediately.

Vegetables

I love walking around the old part of Kirkwall on a quiet summer's evening. As St Magnus Cathedral tolls its curfew, I like to lean over the stone dykes of allotments and admire the dedication and expertise of Kirkwall's vegetable growers. Of course, one needs only to visit a horticultural show in Orkney to realise that quality vegetables are a feature of the whole county.

The variety of vegetables which thrive in Orkney is too great to list here. We all have our favourites, however, and two stand out for me as worthy of special mention.

The first are Orkney tomatoes. Technically fruits, these ripen slowly in windows and hothouses blessed with long summer daylight. They have the perfect blend of sweetness and sharpness and are so good, when compared with imported varieties (which ripen in transit), that they are separately labelled in shops for discerning customers.

The second are Orkney potatoes. Grown in sandy soils, boiled immediately after lifting, dried outside in the fresh Orkney wind and served with local butter, these are, indeed, vegetables fit for a king.

An' they could mak' a banquet wae a heid o' kail

The Auld Hoose Spaeks, C. M. Costie

Clapshot

(serves 4)

To achieve perfect clapshot, use a dry potato such as Golden Wonder or Sharpe's Express which will counteract the wetness of the turnip. In addition, a well frosted turnip will provide your clapshot with better flavour and colour.

---

1 lb (450g) swede (peeled weight)
1¾ lb (800g) potatoes (peeled weight)
1 medium onion, chopped (optional)

salt and pepper
butter

---

1 Cut the swede into very small cubes so they can cook thoroughly while the potatoes are boiling.

2 Place all three vegetables in a pot and just cover with water. Then boil until the potatoes are tender.

3 Strain and dry well on the hob, shaking the pot as you do so.

4 Next add the salt, a generous shake of pepper and the butter.

5 Mash until uniform in colour and serve with mince, sausages, cold meat or haggis.

< Allotments, Kirkwall

Clapshot Croquettes

(makes 24 approximately)

With little extra cost, clapshot is here transformed into something more special.

For the clapshot

12 oz (340g) potatoes (peeled weight)

6 oz (175g) swede, diced small (peeled weight)

1 oz (25g) butter

salt and pepper

½ - 1 level tsp grated nutmeg

For the coating

a little plain flour

2 eggs, beaten

4 oz (110g) dry white breadcrumbs

1 Boil the vegetables together until the potatoes are cooked. Then strain.

2 Next dry them thoroughly on the hob. Add the butter and mash well.

3 Now stir in the seasoning and nutmeg. Allow to cool slightly.

4 Using your hands, roll small amounts in the flour to form cylinders, each the size of a wine cork.

5 Dip each croquette, first in beaten egg and then breadcrumbs. Refrigerate for at least one hour.

6 Fry in hot oil for a few minutes until golden brown. Serve immediately. Alternatively, you may wish to heat these through in a hot oven.

New Potato Bake

(serves 4)

This acts as a main course and needs nothing other than a salad as an accompaniment. With its fullness of flavour, this is certainly one of my tea-time favourites.

2 lb (900g) small new potatoes	a little grated nutmeg
salted water	5 oz (150g) unsmoked bacon, chopped
2 oz (50g) butter	1 tbsp capers
1 oz (25g) plain flour	2 oz (50g) Gouda cheese, grated
15 fl oz (450ml) milk	1 tbsp sesame seeds
pepper	

Preheat oven to 200°C, 180°C for Fan oven, 400°F, Gas Mark 6

1 Clean and scrub the potatoes, cutting the larger ones in half. Boil in salted water until just tender, strain and dry on the hob.

2 While the potatoes are boiling, make a white sauce. First melt the butter in a saucepan. Then stir in the flour and cook for a few moments. Gradually add the milk, stirring continuously. Season with the pepper and nutmeg (but not salt). Add the bacon and capers to the sauce.

3 Next grease an ovenproof dish, large enough to take the potatoes in one layer with a few gaps. Pour over the sauce, poking the bacon and capers into the spaces between the potatoes.

4 Lastly, top with the cheese, sprinkle over the sesame seeds and bake for 25 minutes.

Baked Potatoes with Watercress and Cottage Cheese

(serves 4)

Watercress grows profusely in many Orkney ditches. Choose leaves from plants that are not in flower and that are found in running water.

4 large baking potatoes, scrubbed	3 oz (75g) watercress, washed thoroughly and chopped
a little oil	
1 oz (25g) butter	8 oz (225g) cottage cheese
1 small onion, finely chopped	freshly ground black pepper

Preheat oven to 200°C, 180°C for Fan oven, 400°F, Gas Mark 6

1 Prick the potatoes on all sides with a fork and, using your hands, cover the surface of each one with oil. Bake for about 1¼ to 1½ hours or until cooked through.

2 Meanwhile melt the butter in a pan and soften the onion for a few minutes. Add the watercress and continue to cook for 2 minutes. Then allow to cool.

3 Next stir in the cheese and season with black pepper.

4 Slit the potatoes open and serve each with the cheese mixture.

New Potatoes Paprika

(serves 5-6 as a side vegetable)

I like this with sausages or chops, but it could also form part of a vegetarian meal.
It is best made using small new potatoes.

2 lb (900g) new potatoes, none bigger than an egg	1 tin (400g) chopped tomatoes
3 tbsp oil	3 fl oz (75ml) water
1 large onion, chopped	salt and pepper
1 small green pepper, chopped	5 fl oz (150ml) natural yoghurt
1 clove garlic, finely chopped	chopped parsley, to garnish
1 tbsp paprika	

1 Clean and scrub the potatoes and set aside in fresh water.

2 Then, using a large saucepan, heat the oil and soften the onion for 2-3 minutes. Stir in the pepper, garlic and paprika, cooking these for a further minute.

3 Next add the chopped tomatoes, water and seasoning. Submerge the potatoes in this mixture, cover and cook for 20-25 minutes or until the potatoes are tender. Remove the lid for the last 5 minutes so the sauce can reduce.

4 Serve each helping with a spoonful of yoghurt and some chopped parsley.

Potato Salad in a Mild Mustard Dressing

(serves 6-8 as part of a salad)

The mustard dressing in this recipe makes an interesting change from more
common mayonnaise dressings. Serve hot or cold.

3 lb (1kg 350g) potatoes, peeled if old, scrubbed if new	2 tbsp natural yoghurt
salted water	2 tsp Dijon mustard
3 tbsp mayonnaise	pepper
2 tbsp white wine vinegar	1 tbsp chopped chives

1 Boil the potatoes in the salted water until just tender. Strain and dry thoroughly on the hob. If using old potatoes, chop them into a bowl. If using small new potatoes, leave them whole.

2 Combine the mayonnaise, vinegar, yoghurt, mustard and pepper in a small bowl.

3 Carefully dress the potatoes and sprinkle over the chives. Serve immediately or chill.

Baked Field Mushrooms

(serves 4 as a side vegetable)

At the end of summer, when Orkney's wild mushrooms appear, try this succulent dish, which is so good it can be eaten by itself. You might also like to serve this as a starter.

8 medium field mushrooms	*salt and freshly ground pepper*
1½ oz (35g) butter	*Parmesan cheese*
2 tbsp lemon juice	

Preheat oven to 190°C, 170°C for Fan oven, 375°F, Gas Mark 5

1 Cut most of the stalk from the mushrooms, wipe them but only peel them if they are blemished.

2 Next place them upside down in a greased, ovenproof dish.

3 Dot each mushroom with butter, sprinkle over the lemon juice and season generously.

4 Top with some Parmesan cheese and bake them, uncovered for 20 minutes.

5 Serve the mushrooms with any escaped juices poured over.

Garden Turnip Gratin with Coriander and Lemon

(serves 6 as a side vegetable)

This aromatic dish goes well with roast chicken or pork.

2 lb (900g) garden turnips, peeled and diced	*2 level tsp coriander seeds, crushed*
salt and pepper	*4 oz (110g) white breadcrumbs*
2 cloves garlic, finely chopped	*grated rind of half a lemon*
3 oz (75g) butter	

1 Boil the turnips in salted water until tender. Then strain, season with pepper and keep warm.

2 While they are cooking, gently fry the garlic without browning in the butter. Stir in the coriander for the last minute. Add the breadcrumbs, lemon rind and seasoning, mixing well to absorb the butter.

3 Spread the turnips in a pre-heated, flat ovenproof dish and cover with the breadcrumbs.

4 Savour the aroma as you finish the dish under a hot grill. It is ready to serve when the topping is crisp and brown.

Garden Turnips with Oatmeal Stuffing

(serves 2-4 as a side vegetable)

These look most attractive, almost like mini turnip lanterns, and go well with roasts or cold meat. Choose turnips which are the size of large eggs.

4 small garden turnips, stalks still on	*2 oz (50g) pinhead oatmeal*
1½ oz (35g) butter	*salt and pepper*
2 oz (50g) finely chopped onion	*1 pinch dried thyme*

1 Carefully peel the turnips with a sharp knife, trying to leave the surface as smooth as possible. Leave on the stalks, cutting these across so that only half an inch remains.

2 Slice a lid from each one and, using a teaspoon, scoop out the insides as if you were making small turnip lanterns. Excess turnip can go towards a pot of soup.

3 Next melt the butter in a frying pan and gently cook the onion until soft. Then add the oatmeal, cooking slowly for 1-2 minutes and stirring the mixture continuously. Season lightly and stir in the thyme.

4 Now spoon the oatmeal mixture into the turnip hollows and replace the lids. There should be sufficient stuffing for the lids to sit high above their bases.

5 Steam the turnips for 20-25 minutes or until tender. If you don't have a steamer, use a saucepan with a tight lid and raise the turnips above the water level on a plate.

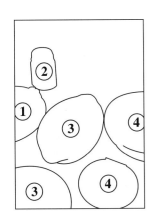

KEY
1   Garden Turnips with Oatmeal Stuffing – *Page 67*
2   Pickled Red Onion Rings – *Page 73*
3   New Potato Bake – *Page 63*
4   Greek Salad, Orkney Style – *Page 70*

Green Cabbage with Vinegar

(serves 4-5 as a side vegetable)

The addition of a little vinegar to cabbage, prior to cooking, intensifies freshness of flavour.

1 green cabbage, about 1½ lb (675g)	2 oz (50g) butter
1 tbsp water	salt
2 tbsp vinegar	pepper

1   Remove the coarse leaves and stalk from the cabbage. Then shred and wash.

2   Put the water, vinegar, butter and salt into a large saucepan. Heat gently to melt the butter.

3   Next add the cabbage and cover tightly. Cook for 10 minutes over a medium heat, stirring occasionally.

4   Before serving, season generously with pepper.

White Cabbage with Gin and Juniper Berries

(serves 4-5 as a side vegetable)

Here is an easy yet special way to serve cabbage. I think the flavours blend admirably.

1 white cabbage, about 1½ lb (675g)	15-16 juniper berries, crushed
3 oz (75g) butter	2 tbsp gin
1 medium onion, thinly sliced	salt and pepper

1   Remove the coarse leaves and stalk from the cabbage. Then shred and wash.

2   Using a large saucepan, melt the butter and soften the onion. Add the juniper berries and gin.

3   Next pile the cabbage on top, season well and mix until it is coated with the gin mixture.

4   Cover and allow the cabbage to cook for about 10 minutes. Stir a couple of times while cooking.

Red Cabbage, Braised with Rum, Pears and Allspice

(serves 5-6 as a side vegetable)

Perfect with roast pork, this winter warmer reheats or freezes without coming to any harm.

1 red cabbage, about 1½ lb (675g)	2 tbsp dark rum
3 fairly hard pears, cored but unpeeled, cut into small pieces	2 tbsp wine vinegar
	1½ tbsp lemon juice
3 medium onions, sliced thinly	1 tbsp oil
1½ oz (35g) demerara sugar	salt and black pepper
1 level tsp allspice	

Preheat oven to 160°C, 140°C for Fan oven, 325°F, Gas Mark 3

1   Remove the outer leaves of the cabbage and cut out the core. Shred finely.

2   Simply combine all the ingredients in a large casserole. Cover and cook for 2½ hours, stirring twice during the cooking time.

Broad Beans with Brown Lentils and Black Butter

(serves 4)

Broad bean growers often have more than they know what to do with. Here's a tasty way to use them up. Serve with some crusty bread as part of a light lunch.

4 oz (110g) whole brown lentils	salt and freshly milled pepper
8 oz (225g) podded broad beans, blanched for one minute in boiling water	3 oz (75g) unsalted butter
	2 tbsp white wine vinegar
1 large carrot, peeled and finely diced	3 tbsp chopped parsley
1 medium onion, finely chopped	

1   Soak the lentils in cold water for 4 hours. Then boil them in unsalted water for 15 minutes, or until just tender, and strain.

2   Meanwhile, boil the beans, carrot and onion for 10 minutes. Strain and mix with the lentils. Season generously.

3   In another saucepan, heat the butter until it is nut-brown in colour (not black). Remove from the heat immediately and stir in the vinegar.

4   Add the parsley and pour over the broad bean mixture.

Mange Tout in Hot Onion Vinaigrette

(serves 4-6 as a side vegetable)

To avoid last minute work, have the mange tout blanched and the onion fried in the butter. This way you'll be able to finish cooking the dish in seconds.

8 oz (225g) mange tout	1 level tsp caster sugar
1 small onion, finely chopped	salt and freshly ground pepper
3 tbsp oil	1 tbsp white wine vinegar

1 Top and tail the mange tout and immerse in boiling water for 60 seconds.

2 Strain quickly and plunge into plenty of iced water. Then remove and pat dry.

3 Next fry the onion in the oil for a few moments. Add the sugar, seasoning, vinegar and mange tout, turning frequently until warmed through.

4 Serve immediately while the mange tout is still crunchy.

Greek Salad, Orkney Style

(serves 6)

The slightly sour quality of some Orkney farm cheese produces an ideal substitute for Feta cheese, one of the ingredients in Greek salad. To combine further the flavours of the Mediterranean and Orkney, try serving this with bere bannocks.

6 oz (175g) Orkney farm cheese, cut into small cubes	2 tbsp black olives
1 small cucumber, sliced	salt and black pepper
6 tomatoes, quartered	1 lemon
	3 tbsp olive oil

1 Mix the cheese, cucumber, tomatoes and olives in a bowl. Then season with the salt and pepper.

2 Cut the lemon in half. Drizzle the juice of one half only over the salad.

3 Next pour over the olive oil and garnish with the remaining lemon, cut into wedges. Serve immediately.

Lettuce and Strawberry Salad

(serves 6 as a side salad)

Two common items from the Orkney garden combine in this recipe with some crunchy walnuts.

For the salad

1 green lettuce (not iceberg)
10 oz (275g) strawberries, hulled and quartered
2 oz (50g) walnuts, broken into small pieces but not crushed

For the dressing

2 tbsp oil (preferably walnut)
1 tbsp cider vinegar
1 tbsp lemon juice
freshly ground white pepper

1 Wash, dry and roughly shred the lettuce. Place in a bowl with the strawberries and nuts.

2 Combine the dressing ingredients and toss the salad in these immediately before serving. If you do this too early, the lettuce will go limp and the strawberries will discolour.

Baked Onions

(serves 4)

Despite the presence of many recipes in cookery books, people seem to shy away from baking onions whole. I include my own version to encourage you to have a go.

4 medium onions, peeled and roots removed
6 fl oz (175ml) white wine
1tbsp tomato sauce
1 level tsp dried mustard
2 tsp sugar

1tbsp vinegar
1 small bay leaf
salt and pepper
1½ oz (35g) butter

Preheat oven to 200°C, 180°C for Fan oven, 400°F, Gas Mark 6

1 Place the onions in a casserole with their root ends on the bottom.

2 Then mix together the wine, tomato sauce, mustard, sugar and vinegar in a small bowl and add this to the casserole. Pop in the bay leaf and season with salt and pepper.

3 Now divide the butter between the four onions, spreading it with a knife over the top of each one.

4 Cover very tightly and bake for 1 hour 15 minutes. Check onions are tender by piercing with a sharp knife.

5 Serve each with a spoonful of sauce poured over.

Onion Flan

(serves 6)

This is a modification of the French 'tarte á l'oignon', with oatmeal pastry instead of the more traditional shortcrust. Serve the flan for lunch or as a starter, with a glass of cool Alsace Riesling.

For the pastry

4 oz (110g) plain flour, sifted
2 oz (50g) fine oatmeal
1½ oz (35g) margarine, cut into small pieces
1½ oz (35g) lard, cut into small pieces
pinch of salt
cold water

For the filling

2 oz (50g) butter
1lb (450g) onions, peeled and thinly sliced
2 large eggs
2 fl oz (50ml) milk
5 fl oz (150ml) single cream
salt and pepper
grated nutmeg

Preheat oven to 200°C, 180°C for Fan oven, 400°F, Gas Mark 6

1 Put all the pastry ingredients except the water into a bowl and rub in the fats until the mixture resembles fine breadcrumbs.

2 Next sprinkle over enough cold water to form a stiff dough. Then chill in the refrigerator.

3 Meanwhile melt the butter in a saucepan and cook the onions slowly until they are soft, stirring frequently to prevent sticking. This should take about 30 minutes.

4 Towards the end of the cooking time, roll out the pastry and use to line an 8-9 inch (20-22cm) flan tin. Prick with a fork.

5 Now beat the eggs lightly and add the milk, cream, seasoning and nutmeg. Spread the onions over the pastry base and pour over the egg mixture.

6 Bake the flan for 30–35 minutes. Remove from the tin and serve lukewarm.

Pickled Red Onion Rings

(for a 2lb or 1kg jar)

This appealingly coloured pickle is easy to make and sweeter than you might imagine.

1¼ lb (560g) red onions, peeled	6 fl oz (175ml) red wine vinegar
4 oz (110g) sugar	1 tsp salt

1 Cut the onions into ¼ inch (½ cm) slices and push out each slice to form rings.

2 Next put the sugar, vinegar and salt into a saucepan and bring to the boil. Check sugar has dissolved.

3 Add the onions and bring back to the boil. Cover and cook for 5 minutes, stirring occassionally. Allow to cool slightly.

4 Preheat the jar, fill with the onion mixture and cover tightly.

Glazed Baby Vegetables in Orkney Butter

(serves 4)

This is perhaps the most colourful vegetable dish you can imagine. Do not feel you have to stick closely to the recipe but, instead, use any small vegetables you have to hand. Cauliflower florets and mange tout are also suitable along with those listed below.

16-20 very small new potatoes, scrubbed	12-16 baby carrots, cleaned but with a small amount of stalk left on
salted water	3-4 oz (75-110g) Orkney butter
1 head of broccoli, broken into florets	2 tsp sugar
8-10 small shallots, peeled	
12-16 radishes, cleaned but with a small amount of stalk left on	

1 Boil the potatoes in salted water until tender. Strain and dry them on the hob.

2 Then blanch the remaining vegetables in boiling salted water for 1–2 minutes only. Strain and refresh in ice cold water. Remove them from the water and pat dry.

3 If desired, the vegetables can be warmed gently, covered, in a moderate oven to speed up the glazing process. Melt the butter in a frying pan and stir in the sugar. When sizzling, add the vegetables in small amounts and turn until warm and shiny. Keep any glazed vegetables warm in the oven while you fry the next batch.

Baked Parsnips with Orkney Cheese

(serves 4-6 as a side vegetable)

Parsnip lovers might like to try this as a main course, where it will serve two or three. A green vegetable is all that you'll need by way of accompaniment.

For the parsnips

2 lb (900g) peeled, sliced parsnips
1 level tsp ground nutmeg
salt and pepper
1 oz (25g) butter

For the topping

1½ oz (35g) butter
1½ oz (35g) plain flour
10 fl oz (300ml) milk
4 oz (110g) coloured Orkney Cheddar, grated
salt and pepper
5 fl oz (150ml) natural yoghurt
1 egg, beaten

Preheat oven to 190°C, 170°C for Fan oven, 375°F, Gas Mark 5

1 First par-boil the parsnips for 5 minutes. Strain and place in a greased ovenproof dish. Sprinkle with nutmeg and seasoning. Then dot with the butter.

2 For the topping, melt the butter in a saucepan. Stir in the flour and cook for a few moments. Gradually add the milk, stirring continuously.

3 Now stir in three quarters of the Cheddar and cook for a few seconds until melted.

4 Remove from the heat, season and mix in the yoghurt. Whisk the beaten egg into the sauce and pour over the parsnips.

5 Finally sprinkle over the remaining cheese and bake for 45 minutes or until bubbling and heated through.

Carrots with Cider and Rosemary

(serves 4-5 as a side vegetable)

The cider and rosemary in this recipe enhance the sweet flavour of fresh young carrots.

1 lb (450g) carrots	½ level tsp rosemary
10 fl oz (300ml) dry cider	2 oz (50g) butter
3tsp soft brown sugar	salt and freshly ground black pepper

1 Peel the carrots, wash them and cut them into lengths or slices (about 1cm thick).

2 Place them in a saucepan and add all the other ingredients. Bring the contents to the boil, give a quick stir and cover.

3 Now reduce the heat and simmer for 12-15 minutes, stirring occasionally.

4 Remove the carrots with a slotted spoon and keep them warm in a serving dish.

5 Then turn up the heat and allow the cider to reduce to a syrupy consistency. Pour over the carrots and serve.

Beetroot with Lime

(serves 4 as a side vegetable)

In this recipe sharp flavoured limes replace the oranges of more traditional beetroot dishes. If you can't get limes, try lemons, but use half the amount.

1 lb (450g) evenly sized beetroot	3 tsp sugar
salted water	1 oz (25g) butter
juice and zest of one lime	1 slice from the above lime, to garnish

1 Wash the beetroot very carefully and trim off most of the stalks, leaving on the tapering roots.

2 Boil the beetroot in salted water until tender. Small beetroot will take about ½-1 hour. Larger beetroot may take 1-2 hours.

3 When the beetroot is cooked, strain and allow to cool slightly. Slip off the skins and dice the insides.

4 Now, using a saucepan, heat the juice and zest of the lime along with the sugar and butter. Allow to sizzle for a few seconds. Then reheat the beetroot in this mixture, stirring frequently.

5 Pile into a dish, garnish with a twist of lime and serve with pork or ham.

Spiced Leeks

(serves 4-5 as a side vegetable)

You can make life easier by slicing the leeks in this recipe but I think serving them in tubular form is much more appealing. Timing is crucial, however, as leeks collapse and lose their attractive appearance quickly.

3 medium leeks, coarse leaves and roots removed	½ level tsp cumin
2 oz (50g) butter	salt and freshly ground black pepper
1 level tsp turmeric	5 fl oz (150ml) water

1 Cut the leeks into 2 inch (5cm) lengths and wash them thoroughly. Dry them with a tea towel or kitchen paper.

2 Next melt the butter in a frying pan and gently fry the spices for a few seconds.

3 Then add the leeks and roll them around to coat them in the butter.

4 Add the seasoning and water. Put a lid on the pan and cook for about 15 minutes or until just tender. Turn the leeks occasionally to ensure they cook evenly.

5 Serve the leeks with the spicy butter poured over.

Celery with Cashew Nuts

(serves 4-6 as a side vegetable)

The protein content in this vegetable recipe makes it highly suitable for vegetarians. The celery also works well when served with any hot or cold roast meat.

1 lb (450g) celery, trimmed of leaves and roots	1 heaped tsp sugar
2 oz (50g) butter	freshly ground black pepper
2 fl oz (50ml) white wine	3½ oz (100g) cashew nuts
1 bay leaf	3 tsp balsamic vinegar

1 Wash the celery and cut into 1 inch (2 cm) pieces. Then melt the butter in a saucepan and cook the celery in this for 5 minutes, stirring frequently.

2 Next add the wine, bay leaf, sugar and a generous amount of black pepper. Cover the saucepan and allow to simmer for 10 minutes, stirring from time to time to ensure even cooking.

3 After that add the nuts and vinegar. Replace the saucepan cover and cook for a further 5 minutes.

Cauliflower with Two Orkney Cheeses and Shallots

(serves 2 for a main course, 4-6 as a side vegetable)

Try this interesting alternative to the more traditional cauliflower and cheese sauce
and you won't be disappointed.

1 cauliflower, 1 lb 4 oz (560g), cut into florets	salt and pepper
2 oz (50g) butter	a little grated nutmeg
2-3 shallots, finely chopped	1 level tsp sugar
1 rounded tbsp plain flour	1 egg, separated
10 fl oz (300ml) milk	2 oz (50g) coloured Orkney Cheddar, grated.
4 oz (110g) Orkney farmhouse cheese, crumbled or grated	

Preheat oven to 200°C, 180°C for Fan oven, 400°F, Gas Mark 6

1 Boil or steam the cauliflower until 'al dente'. Strain and place in a large, flat ovenproof dish.

2 While the cauliflower is cooking, melt half the butter in a saucepan and soften the shallots for a few minutes. Then remove them to a dish.

3 In the same saucepan, melt the rest of the butter. Stir in the flour and allow to cook for a few moments. Gradually add the milk, stirring continuously.

4 Now add the farmhouse cheese, seasoning, nutmeg and sugar. Continue to stir until the cheese has melted. Return the shallots to the saucepan and stir in the egg yolk. Cover with a layer of clingfilm to prevent a skin forming and set aside.

5 Meanwhile whisk the egg white until it forms floppy peaks.

6 When you are ready to cook the dish, remove the clingfilm from the sauce and fold in the egg white.

7 Pour this over the cauliflower and top with the grated Cheddar.

8 Bake for 20-25 minutes or until cooked through and bubbling.

Meat

It is hard to imagine a better meat product anywhere in the world than Orkney beef. Its richness and tenderness are the themes of universal admiration. The farmer's care of his animals together with high standards of both breeding and feeding all contribute to this paramount quality.

One of the great treats of the summer dinner table in Orkney is the appearance of new season lamb. With its succulence and subtle flavour, this is the perfect accompaniment to new Orkney potatoes which, by a happy coincidence, arrive at the same time.

Among the remaining meats found in our isles are free-range pork, domestic foul, rabbits and game birds. Together with beef and lamb the range of recipes which stem from these is, as you can imagine, endless. Without leaving the county for ingredients, Orcadians can certainly provide meat courses which are rich in diversity.

We'll drive around in
Humber Snipes
and smoke a fat cigar.
And tell the world it's
Orkney Beef
that made us what we are.

George Corrigall

Beef and Oyster Pie

(serves 6-8)

Made from two of Orkney's best products, cooked together in a rich, red wine sauce and topped with golden, puff pastry, this makes an impressive centrepiece to a dinner party.

2 lb (900g) stewing beef, cubed		1 tsp dried mustard
2 tbsp plain flour		salt and pepper
3 tbsp oil		2 medium onions, sliced
2 tbsp brandy		4 oz (110g) mushrooms, sliced
15 fl oz (450ml) red wine		6-8 oysters, shelled
2 bay leaves		1 lb (450g) puff pastry, defrosted if frozen
1 level tsp dried thyme		1 egg, beaten

Preheat oven to 215°C, 200°C for Fan oven, 425°F, Gas Mark 7

1 Coat the beef in the flour and fry, a few pieces at a time, in very hot oil until dark brown on all sides. Set the beef aside.

2 Add a little more oil to the pan, if required, and stir in any flour that remains.

3 Then pour in the brandy and set alight. When the flames have died down, gradually add the wine, stirring as you do so.

4 Next put the meat in a saucepan and pour over the red wine mixture. Add the herbs, mustard, seasoning and onions. Mix well and cover tightly.

5 Cook for 2 hours over a low heat, checking that the contents do not stick to the bottom of the pan. Add the mushrooms for the last 2 minutes. Remove bay leaves.

6 Now pour the meat mixture into a 3-4 pint (1¾-2¼ litre) pie dish. Allow to cool. Add a splash more wine if the mixture is too thick.

7 Make six to eight hollows between the cubes of meat and fill these with the oysters and their juice.

8 Roll out the pastry to fit your pie dish. Seal the edges and cut a hole in the centre.

9 Brush with the beaten egg and bake for 25–30 minutes.

< Beef and Oyster Pie

Beef in Dark Island Ale with Oatmeal and Mustard Doughboys

(serves 4)

The Dark Islands Ale lends a nutty, full-flavoured quality to this casserole. It is a good choice for a winter dinner party.

For the casserole

3 tbsp oil
1½ lb (675g) stewing steak, cubed
1 level tbsp plain flour
1 pint (600ml) Dark Island
2 medium onions, sliced
2 cloves garlic, crushed
2 tsp sugar
1 tbsp wine vinegar
1 bay leaf
salt and black pepper
3 oz (75g) button mushrooms, sliced

For the doughboys

2 oz (50g) self-raising flour
3 oz (75g) medium oatmeal
2 oz (50g) shredded suet
1 small onion, chopped
1 heaped tsp English mustard
3-4 fl oz (75-100ml) water

Preheat oven to 190°C, 175°C for Fan oven, 375°F, Gas Mark 5

1 Heat the oil in a frying pan and sear the meat, a few pieces at a time, until dark brown on all sides. Remove the meat to a large casserole.

2 Next add the flour to the pan, pouring in a little more oil if necessary. Allow to cook for a minute before adding the beer, a little at a time.

3 Now add the onions, garlic, sugar, vinegar, bay leaf and seasoning. Bring to boiling point and pour over the meat in the casserole.

4 Cover very tightly with a lid and baking foil, and cook for 1¾ hours in the oven.

5 Meanwhile make the doughboys by mixing together all the ingredients in a bowl. Then, using floured hands and a floured work surface, form the mixture into 8 balls.

6 After the casserole has cooked for 1¾ hours, stir in the mushrooms and place the doughboys on top. Return to the oven for a final 30 minutes, still covered.

7 Remove the bay leaf before serving. Allow 2 doughboys per person.

Salted, Spiced Brisket of Beef

(serves 8)

If you want an unusual but unpretentious centre to a meal, then this is for you. There may be more work involved than in simply boiling beef, but I think it's worth the effort.

2½ lb (1kg 125g) boned, unrolled brisket	*½ level tsp ground mace*
6 oz (175g) salt	*½ level tsp ground allspice*
20 black peppercorns, crushed	*1 bay leaf, finely chopped*
20 juniper berries, crushed	*½ small onion, finely chopped*
½ level tsp ground nutmeg	*1 oz (25g) muscovado sugar*
½ level tsp ground cloves	*½ level tsp saltpetre (from chemists)*

1 Trim the meat of most of its fat, wipe and place in a large, flat dish. Cover on all sides with the salt, rubbing in well. Then put in the fridge for 24 hours.

2 Next day, pour off any juices which have gathered and rub all the other ingredients into the meat, along with any salt remaining in the bottom of the dish.

3 Return to the fridge for 4 more days, turning the meat occasionally, rubbing it with any spice mixture which remains and draining off any liquid which has formed.

4 Next roll the brisket tightly and secure firmly with 4 or 5 pieces of string.

5 Using a large saucepan, cover the meat with water and simmer for 3 hours. Allow to cool in the water for 1 hour.

6 Now remove the meat and press it between 2 plates with a weight on top.

7 After at least 10 hours pressing, slice the meat thinly and serve cold with a hot potato salad.

Sirloin Steak with Whisky and Ginger Sauce

(serves 2)

Made from good Orkney beef, this is quick, easy and perfect for a romantic dinner for two.

2 sirloin steaks	2 tbsp whisky
a little oil	3 tbsp double cream
1 level tbsp finely chopped, fresh ginger	salt and freshly ground black pepper
1 clove garlic, finely chopped	

1 Using a frying pan, heat just enough oil to cover the surface, until smoking hot. Then sear the steaks for a minute on each side. Reduce the heat and cook the steaks to your own taste. Remove them from the pan and keep them warm.

2 Gently fry the ginger and garlic for one minute in the same pan. Add the whisky and allow to sizzle.

3 Then pour in the cream, stir and simmer for a moment. Season well and serve with the steaks.

Alan's Tip:

"To peel garlic cloves more easily, first crush them roughly by pressing them with the side of a large bladed knife."

Savoury Mince with Root Vegetable Topping

(serves 6)

Here is a Shepherd's Pie with a difference. Packed full of the loveliest flavours, this
is the perfect dish for a cold winter's day.

1½ lb (675g) best mince	1 fl oz (25ml) water
1 tbsp oil	2 lb (900g) potatoes (peeled weight)
1 tin (400g) tomatoes	1 lb (450g) diced swede
1 medium onion, sliced	2 medium carrots, peeled and chopped
1 tbsp tomato purée	1 medium parsnip, peeled and chopped
2 bay leaves	1 oz (25g) butter
pinch of rosemary	grated nutmeg
salt and pepper	

Preheat oven to 200°C, 180°C for Fan oven, 400°F, Gas Mark 6

1 Brown the mince in the oil, stirring from time to time.

2 Then add the tomatoes, onion, tomato purée, herbs, seasoning and water. Chop the tomatoes and cover tightly. Simmer for 45 minutes.

3 Meanwhile, boil the 4 root vegetables together until the potatoes are cooked. Strain, reserving the stock for a pot of soup.

4 Dry the vegetables thoroughly on the hob and add the butter, nutmeg and more seasoning. Mash until the carrot appears as flecks in the mixture.

5 Next put the mince in the bottom of a large, flat, ovenproof dish.

6 Top with the mashed vegetables and bake for 30 minutes, or until bubbling and golden. Allow 40 minutes in the oven if cooking from cold.

Steamed Mince Pudding

(serves 8)

A simple alternative to steak and kidney pudding, this makes a hearty meal when served with winter vegetables.

10 oz (275g) self-raising flour	1½ lb (675g) best mince
5 oz (150g) shredded suet	1 medium onion, finely sliced
salt and pepper	2 level tbsp plain flour
cold water	1 heaped tsp dried mustard

1 Mix the self-raising flour, suet and seasoning with enough cold water to form a dough that leaves the bowl clean.

2 Grease a 2½ pint (1½ litre) pudding basin thoroughly and line the bottom with a circle of greaseproof paper. This will ensure your pudding turns out without breaking.

3 Remove one quarter of the dough and roll the rest into a circle. Use this to line the pudding basin.

4 Mix the mince, onion, plain flour and mustard together with some more salt and pepper.

5 Then fill the pastry-lined basin loosely with this mixture, adding enough cold water to reach almost to the top.

6 Now roll out the remaining dough to form a lid. Dampen the edges and seal well.

7 Cover with 2 sheets of foil and secure with string. Remember to leave a wide pleat in the foil as the pudding will expand while cooking.

8 Steam for 5 hours, keeping an eye on the water level.

9 To serve, remove the foil and slide a knife round the edges of the pudding. Invert onto a plate and remove the greaseproof paper.

< Steamed Mince Pudding

Stuffed Meatballs in Tomato Sauce

(serves 5-6)

These are a bit fiddly to make, but well worth the effort when your guests discover that each meatball has some delicious Orkney Cheddar at its centre.

For the meatballs

1¼ lbs (560g) best minced beef
3 oz (75g) white breadcrumbs
1 small onion, finely chopped
2 cloves garlic, finely chopped
1 level tsp dried oregano
1 egg, beaten
salt and pepper
5 oz (150g) Orkney Cheddar
plain flour
a little oil

For the sauce

1 oz (25g) butter
1 medium onion, chopped
1 small green pepper, deseeded and chopped
1 clove garlic, finely chopped
2 tins (each 400g) tomatoes
1 level tsp dried oregano
salt and pepper
1 tsp sugar

Preheat oven to 200°C, 180°C for Fan oven, 400°F, Gas Mark 6

1 Begin by mixing the mince, breadcrumbs, onion, garlic, oregano, egg and seasoning in a large bowl.

2 Divide the mixture into 2, then 4 and so on until you have 32 small piles.

3 In the same way cut the cheese into 32 small cubes.

4 Then flatten the meat piles and place a cube of cheese on each. Roll them into balls between your palms, making sure the cheese is well sealed in the meat.

5 Now coat the meatballs with flour and brown them, a few at a time, in the oil.

6 To make the sauce, melt the butter in a saucepan and sweat the onion until soft, adding the green pepper and garlic for the last 2 minutes.

7 Thoroughly chop the tomatoes and add them to the saucepan along with the oregano, seasoning and sugar. Cover and simmer for 5 minutes.

8 Next place the meatballs, a few at a time, in a large casserole, pouring over the tomato sauce between each addition.

9 Cover tightly and bake for 1 hour. Serve with spaghetti or tagliatelle.

Curried Beef Sausages

(serves 4-6)

Orkney beef sausages are lovely spiced up in this easy curry.

a little oil

1½ lb (675g) beef sausages, pricked

1 medium large onion, chopped

1 rounded tsp curry powder (or your own spice
  mixture)

1 large cooking apple, peeled and cored

15 fl oz (450ml) water

2 oz (50g) sultanas

salt and pepper

1 Using a little oil to prevent sticking, lightly brown the sausages in a frying pan. Then remove them to a plate and discard almost all the fat.

2 In what remains, cook the onion until soft but not brown. Add the curry powder and fry gently for a minute, stirring occasionally.

3 Then grate the apple and add this to the onion mixture.

4 Pour over the water, stir in the sultanas and season well.

5 Now return the sausages to the pan and cover tightly.

6 Simmer for 20-25 minutes. Serve with boiled rice.

Spiced Beefburgers

(makes 8-9)

For a change, try these tasty burgers next time you barbecue. They are popular with children and adults alike.

1½ lb (675g) best minced beef

2 oz (50g) white breadcrumbs

2 garlic gloves, finely chopped

1 inch (2½ cm) piece of root ginger, peeled and
  finely chopped

½ to ¾ tsp hot chilli powder, depending on taste

salt and pepper

4 tbsp chopped parsley

1 Simply mix together all the ingredients and divide into 8 or 9 portions.

2 Press into burger shapes and barbecue (or grill) until browned and cooked through.

Beef Olives

(serves 4)

Orkney butcher shops sell excellent beef olives but you might like to try this recipe for the extra satisfaction it involves. The inclusion of red wine and some exotic vegetables produces a rich end product.

2 medium onions, peeled	4 medium carrots, chunked
2 oz (50g) butter	10 fl oz (300ml) beef stock
4 oz (110g) white breadcrumbs	5 fl oz (150ml) red wine
2 tbsp fresh parsley, chopped	1 small yellow or red pepper, pith removed, deseeded and chopped
½ level tsp dried thyme	
4 tbsp milk	2 medium courgettes, sliced
salt and pepper	beurre manié (1 tbsp plain flour mixed with 1 tbsp soft margarine)
1lb (450g) topside, thinly sliced	

Preheat oven to 180°C, 165°C for Fan oven, 350°F, Gas Mark 4

1 Begin by finely dicing one of the onions and softening it in butter for 3-4 minutes. Then stir in the breadcrumbs, herbs, milk and seasoning. Allow to cool completely.

2 Next divide the mixture between the meat slices and roll them up to enclose the stuffing. You can secure each with string but I find this unnecessary with larger slices.

3 Place the meat parcels in a greased, roomy casserole. Add the carrots and the remaining onion, which should be sliced.

4 Bring the stock and wine to boiling point and pour into the casserole.

5 Cover very tightly with a layer of cooking foil and a lid, and cook for 1½ hours.

6 Add the pepper and courgettes, and give a final 30 minutes cooking time.

7 Now remove the casserole from the oven and pour the stock into a saucepan. Bring to simmering point and gradually whisk in the beurre manié.

8 Allow to cook gently for 2-3 minutes and season to taste.

9 Serve the beef olives with the vegetables and the thickened sauce poured over.

Summer Lamb Casserole

(serves 6)

Made from tender, young lamb and sweet, summer vegetables, this has to be one
of the best casseroles I have ever tasted.

1½ lb (675g) stewing lamb, cubed	1 tin (400g) tomatoes, thoroughly chopped
plain flour	1 medium onion, chopped
a little oil	salt and pepper
10 oz (275g) garden turnips, peeled and chunked	a little dill seed (optional)
6 oz (175g) young carrots, scrubbed	4 oz (110g) mushrooms, sliced
2 glasses white wine	1 large courgette, sliced
8 fl oz (225ml) water	

Preheat oven to 190°C, 170°C for Fan oven, 375°F, Gas Mark 5

1 Coat the lamb in the flour and sear, a few cubes at a time, in hot oil.

2 In a large casserole, mix the meat with all the other ingredients, except the mushrooms and courgette. Cover tightly and bake for 1½ hours.

3 Now remove the casserole from the oven and stir in the mushrooms and courgette.

4 Cover again and cook for a further 30 minutes.

5 As with any summer casserole, this is lovely with new Orkney potatoes.

91

Lamb Chops with Mint Sauce and Almonds

(serves 4)

The last thing delicate, young lamb needs as an accompaniment is the harsh taste of mint sauce from a jar. Here is a much milder version, which complements lamb beautifully and which also has the added texture of crunchy flaked almonds.

2 oz (50g) butter

8 small lamb chops (or 4 large)

1½ oz (35g) flaked almonds

half a medium onion, finely chopped

2 tbsp white wine vinegar

5 fl oz (150ml) double cream

3 level tbsp chopped fresh mint

salt and pepper

sprigs of fresh mint (to garnish)

1 Melt the butter in a frying pan and cook the chops on both sides to your taste. Remove the meat and keep warm.

2 Now fry the almonds until light brown, removing them quickly before they burn. Keep warm.

3 Then cook the onion until soft. Add the vinegar, cream and mint. Boil for 1 minute, stirring continuously and season with the salt and pepper.

4 Arrange the lamb chops on 4 plates and pour the sauce around. Sprinkle over the flaked almonds and garnish with the sprigs of fresh mint.

Minced Lamb and Peanut Kebabs

(makes 14-16)

You can cook these as sausages if you don't have skewers. They freeze well, so you can make a supply ready for last minute barbecues.

1 lb (450g) minced lamb

1 oz (25g) white breadcrumbs

1 small onion, finely chopped

6 oz (175g) salted peanuts, crushed

2 tbsp chopped chives

pepper

juice and rind of half a lemon

1 Mix together all the ingredients in a bowl.

2 Then divide the mixture into 14 to 16 portions and mould these with your hands into sausage shapes.

3 Now thread the sausages onto greased skewers and press them firmly. If you have long skewers, you will get 2 or 3 on each.

4 Barbecue (or grill) the kebabs until browned on all sides and cooked through.

Lamb's Liver with Herbed Barley

(serves 4)

Serve herbed, buttered barley in place of potatoes in this easy dish. Some steamed broccoli florets are all you'll need by way of accompaniment.

2 oz (50g) pearl barley	12 fl oz (350ml) water
1 medium onion, chopped	1lb (450g) lamb's liver, sliced
3 medium carrots, peeled and diced	seasoned plain flour
¼ level tsp dried thyme	oil
½ level tsp dried mustard	2 oz (50g) butter
3 rashers bacon, chopped	1 rounded tbsp chopped, fresh parsley
salt and pepper	1 level tbsp snipped, fresh chives

1 Put the barley, onion, carrots, thyme, mustard, bacon, seasoning and water into a saucepan and cook, covered, for about 35-40 minutes, or until the barley is tender and the liquid has been absorbed.

2 Meanwhile, dip the liver in seasoned flour and fry on both sides, in hot oil, until the blood stops flowing. Do not overcook, otherwise the liver will be tough. Try to time things so that the barley and liver are ready about the same time.

3 Just before serving, stir the butter into the barley until it melts. Then mix in the fresh herbs.

4 Serve the liver on a bed of barley, surrounded by broccoli.

Pork and Apricot Meat Loaf

(serves 6)

Serve this sweet and sour meat loaf cold with a salad in summer or hot with cooked vegetables in winter.

1½ lb (675g) pork mince	2 tbsp brown sugar
3 oz (75g) white breadcrumbs	2 tbsp soy sauce
1 medium onion, chopped	3 tbsp vinegar
8 oz (225g) dried apricots, chopped	2 tbsp tomato sauce
2 eggs, beaten	salt and pepper

Preheat oven to 190°C, 175°C for Fan oven, 375°F, Gas Mark 5

1 Simply mix all the ingredients thoroughly in a large bowl.

2 Then grease a 2 lb (1kg) loaf tin and pack with the mixture.

3 Cover loosely with a layer of foil and bake for 1 hour 15 minutes.

4 Slide a knife round the edges before turning out.

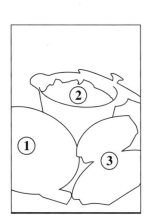

KEY
1   Pork and Apricot Meatloaf – *Page 95*
2   Summer Lamb Casserole – *Page 91*
3   Duck Stir Fry – *Page 101*

Pork Stew with Prunes and Apples

(serves 4-5)

Pork is, in my opinion, the meat which marries best with fruit flavours. Try this delicious stew and I'm sure you'll agree.

1½ lb (675g) stewing pork, cubed	½ level tsp dried sage
a little oil	10 oz (275g) prunes, stoned (use the type which requires no soaking)
1 medium onion, sliced	
10 fl oz (300ml) chicken stock	2 dessert apples, cored and diced, but not peeled
salt and pepper	3 tbsp fromage frais

1 Sear the pork on all sides, in hot oil, a few cubes at a time.

2 Then cook the onion for a few minutes in any oil that remains.

3 Pour off excess fat and return the pork cubes to the pan. Add the stock, seasoning and sage.

4 Bring to simmering point, cover tightly and cook gently for 1 hour 45 minutes.

5 Next add the prunes and apples. Bring back to simmering point and cook for a further 15 minutes. If you want your stew to reduce, leave the lid off for this time.

6 Just before serving, stir in the fromage frais and reheat gently.

Sweet and Sour Pork Sausages

(serves 4-5)

You can jazz up sausages with very little effort by following this recipe.
Serve with buttered noodles or boiled rice.

1 lb 4 oz (560g) pork sausages, pricked	2 tbsp soy sauce
1 rounded tbsp cornflour	3 tbsp vinegar
1½ tbsp sugar	1 level tbsp tomato purée
5 fl oz (150ml) cold water	1 small tin (220g) pineapple, chopped but not strained
3 tsp Worcestershire sauce	

1 Grill the sausages under a medium heat until cooked on all sides.

2 Meanwhile stir the cornflour, sugar and water together in a saucepan until evenly blended. Add all the other ingredients, including the pineapple juice.

3 Then heat gently until thickened, stirring continuously.

4 Add the cooked sausages to the sweet and sour sauce, and stir to coat them. Simmer briefly and serve.

Kale and Pork and Tatties

(serves 6)

Originally this would have been made using dried, salt pork, in which case the meat was soaked overnight prior to cooking. Nowadays, a bacon joint or fresh pork knee is often substituted. Cooking all three ingredients in one pot produces a lovely, waxy quality in the potatoes and a wholesome stock for soup next day.

1¾ lb (800g) bacon joint (or salt pork, presoaked)

water

2½ lb (1kg 125g) potatoes (peeled weight)

1½ lb (675g) white or green cabbage, stalk removed and shredded

freshly ground pepper

melted butter

---

1 Put the bacon in a roomy pot and almost cover with water. Put on a lid, bring to the boil and cook for 1½ hours.

2 Then add the potatoes and cabbage. Return to boiling point and cook until the potatoes are just tender.

3 Drain off the liquid (reserving it for soup) and season with pepper.

4 Carve the bacon and serve with melted butter poured over the potatoes and cabbage.

County Show Night Chicken

(serves 4)

This is so good you'll never want to go out on County Show Night again. Its wholesomeness suitably counteracts any 'bruck' eaten earlier at the Show.

4 medium chicken fillets, skinned	*1½ oz (35g) chopped, mixed nuts*
1 clove garlic, halved	*2 oz (50g) white breadcrumbs*
3 oz (75g) butter	*salt and freshly ground pepper*
6 oz (175g) white Orkney Cheddar, grated	

Preheat oven to 180°C, 160°C for Fan oven, 350°F, Gas Mark 4

1 Rub the chicken surface all over with the garlic halves.

2 Then place the fillets, side by side, in a greased, flat ovenproof dish. Dot with one third of the butter and cover with the grated cheese.

3 Using a frying pan, melt the remaining butter. Add the nuts and breadcrumbs. Gently fry until the butter is evenly absorbed and season well.

4 At this point you can go to the County Show, secure in the knowledge that your main course is well underway.

5 After the show, cook the chicken, uncovered, for 15 minutes. Then remove from the oven and press the breadcrumb mixture over each portion. Return the dish to the oven for 45 minutes, or until cooked enough.

6 Serve with new Orkney potatoes and a green salad.

KEY
1   Lettuce and Strawberry Salad – *Page 71*
2   County Show Night Chicken – *Page 99*

Mock Cockie Chicken

(serves 4)

At one time young, male chickens frequently provided a tender stew for Orcadian families. Although now a rare commodity, you can relive this nostalgic taste in the following recipe.

4 chicken quarters, skinned

1 oz (25g) butter, preferably Orkney farmhouse

15 fl oz (450ml) chicken stock

3 tbsp chopped chives

salt and white pepper

4 heaped tsp cornflour

2 fl oz (50ml) milk

1 Fry the chicken gently on both sides in the butter until lightly browned. Pour over the stock.

2 Then stir in two tablespoons of the chives along with the seasoning.

3 Cover and simmer for 45 minutes, or until cooked.

4 Meanwhile, using a small bowl, mix the cornflour and milk to form a smooth consistency.

5 When the chicken is cooked, remove the quarters and keep warm. Stir the cornflour and milk into the stock to thicken. Cook gently for a few moments.

6 Remove from the heat and add the last tablespoon of chives.

7 Serve the chicken with the sauce and new potatoes.

Duck Stir Fry
(serves 2)

You can make this colourful dish using domestic duck but, if you have a gamey palate, wild duck is even better.

2 tbsp sunflower oil

½ inch (1cm) root ginger, chopped finely

½ red chilli, deseeded and chopped finely

1 clove garlic, crushed

2 shallots, finely chopped

1 duck breast (or 2 wild duck breasts), skinned and cut into thin strips

½ tbsp honey

2 tbsp rich soy sauce

1 tbsp sherry

3 oz (75g) mange tout

1 small red pepper, pith removed, deseeded, and cut into thin strips

1 medium carrot, peeled and cut into thin strips

3 oz (75g) bean sprouts

2 spring onions chopped finely

freshly ground black pepper

1 Heat the oil in a wok or large frying pan and fry the ginger, chilli, garlic and shallots for a few moments.

2 Then add the duck and cook over a high heat for 2-3 minutes.

3 Now stir in the honey, soy sauce and sherry. Put the mange tout, red pepper and carrot on top of the duck, cover and allow to steam for about 2 minutes.

4 Remove the cover and add the bean sprouts, spring onions and pepper. Stir briefly to heat these ingredients and serve immediately with a few noodles, if desired.

Stovies
(serves 4)

This is a good way to use up left-over meat. Keep the dish as dry as possible, only adding a splash of water, now and again, to stop the mixture sticking.

3 oz (75g) butter

2 medium onions, sliced

2½ lb (1kg 125g) peeled potatoes, sliced fairly thickly

2 medium carrots, peeled and sliced

salt and pepper

4 fl oz (100ml) water (approximately)

12 oz (340g) cooked meat (approximately)

a little left-over gravy (optional)

1 Melt the butter in a large saucepan and soften the onions for a few minutes.

2 Then add the potatoes, carrots and a generous amount of seasoning. Cook over a gentle heat for approximately 40 minutes or until the potatoes are tender but not soft. Keep covered during cooking and add a splash of water if the mixture begins to stick. Stir occasionally to ensure even cooking.

3 When you think the potatoes are nearly ready, add the meat and gravy (if used) for the last 5 minutes.

Desserts

*W*ithout much consideration, you might expect a dearth of Orcadian ingredients in this section of the book. You would be wrong, however, as there is a wealth of local fare at our fingertips.

The climate of Orkney enables three fruits, in particular, to prosper — strawberries, gooseberries and rhubarb. Some gardeners produce healthy crops of blackcurrants, redcurrants and raspberries, usually in sheltered gardens, whilst greenhouses may supply surprisingly exotic fruits for our northern latitude.

Let us not overlook puddings which can be made without the use of fruit, whilst still adhering to local ingredients. Rich cream and milk, farm cheese and flavourings such as malt whisky, fudge and honey all have their part to play in the Orcadian dessert course.

For festive fare or birthday treat, a clootie dumpling's hard to beat.

Harvey Johnston

Clootie Dumpling

(For a 5lb or 2¼ kg dumpling)

This is an old recipe from the island of Sanday. When I was given it, I also received several tips on how to achieve perfect results. I include these in the recipe below. The end product is magic!

1½ lb (675g) plain flour, sifted	2 tbsp syrup
6 oz (175g) hard margarine, cut into pieces	1 oz (25g) mixed peel
3 level tsp baking soda	6 oz (175g) sultanas
3 level tsp dried ginger	6 oz (175g) raisins
3 level tsp cinnamon	3 oz (75g) currants
3 level tsp mixed spice	2 small eggs, beaten
1 level tsp ground cloves	milk to mix
10 oz (275g) sugar	caster sugar and plain flour (for the cloth)
2 tbsp treacle	

1 Put the flour into a large bowl and rub in the margarine until the mixture resembles breadcrumbs.

2 Then stir in the soda, spices, sugar, treacle, syrup, peel, fruit and beaten eggs. Add enough milk to create a consistency between sticky and dropping.

3 Next scald a pudding cloth and lay it out on the table. Dust evenly with a layer of caster sugar followed by a layer of plain flour. Do this for an area bigger than the base of the pudding so that a skin can form on the sides and top.

4 Place the pudding mixture in the middle of the cloth and dust lightly with some more flour. Draw up the sides and secure tightly with a piece of string (not nylon string, as this slips). Allow 1-2 inches (2½-5cm) between the pudding and the top of the cloth to let the mixture expand.

5 Now put the pudding, with the knot uppermost, into a pot of boiling water. The pot should be about the same diameter as the pudding and should have fairly high sides. Set a plate in the bottom of the pot to keep the pudding from too fierce a heat.

6 Boil for 4 hours, topping up regularly with boiling water. Do not allow to boil dry.

7 When cooked, remove the cloth and serve hot with custard or cream. Alternatively allow to cool and serve slices with tea or coffee.

< Orkney Fruits

Rhubarb Fruit Sponge

(serves 6)

Rhubarb combines well with other fruit flavours in this pudding. Try it on a cool day in early summer while the rhubarb is still young.

12 oz (340g) rhubarb, washed and cut into ½ inch (1 cm) lengths	4 oz (110g) soft margarine
2 oz (50g) muscovado sugar	4 oz (110g) caster sugar
juice of one orange	2 oz (50g) plain flour, sifted
1 level tsp ground ginger	2 eggs, separated
2 bananas, peeled and sliced	grated rind of one orange
1½ oz (35g) sultanas	5 fl oz (150ml) milk

Preheat oven to 170°C, 150°C for Fan oven, 325°F, Gas Mark 3

1 Place the rhubarb in a saucepan along with the muscovado sugar, orange juice and ginger.

2 Bring to the boil and simmer for 2-3 minutes, stirring occasionally. Then add the bananas and sultanas.

3 Now cream the margarine with the caster sugar. Beat in the flour, egg yolks, orange rind and lastly the milk, a little at a time.

4 Whisk the egg whites in a separate bowl until they form floppy peaks. Using a metal spoon, carefully fold these into the sponge mixture.

5 Reheat the contents of the saucepan until they are simmering. Then pour them into a large, greased casserole.

6 Cover the fruit and rhubarb with the sponge mixture and bake for 45-50 minutes. Serve immediately with a jug of cream.

Luxury Rhubarb and Apple Crumble

(serves 8)

The addition of brandy, butter, egg yolks and cream gives a beautiful, rich quality
to this pudding.

For the filling

1 lb (450g) rhubarb, washed and cut into ½ inch (1 cm) lengths
2 cooking apples, peeled, cored and sliced
3 oz (75g) sugar
1 tsp grated nutmeg
3 tbsp brandy
2 oz (50g) butter
2 egg yolks
2 tbsp cream (top of the milk will do)

For the crumble

10 oz (275g) plain flour
6 oz (175g) butter
4 oz (110g) granulated sugar
1 oz (25g) demerara sugar

Preheat oven to 190°C, 170°C for Fan oven, 375°F, Gas Mark 5

1 In an uncovered saucepan, cook the rhubarb, apples, sugar and nutmeg with one tablespoon water until the fruit is soft. Stir occasionally to ensure even cooking.

2 Then whisk in the brandy and the butter. Set aside to cool slightly.

3 Meanwhile, whisk the egg yolks with the cream in a small bowl. Add this to the cooled rhubarb mixture and whisk until smooth.

4 In another bowl, make the crumble by sifting the flour and rubbing in the butter. Then stir in the granulated sugar.

5 To assemble, pour the rhubarb mixture into a large greased casserole. Spoon the crumble evenly on top and sprinkle with the demerara sugar.

6 Bake for 40-45 minutes and serve with cream.

Bottled Gooseberries

(for a 2 lb or 1kg jar)

Serve these summer delights with cream or Orkney ice cream. The fact that the gooseberries have been bottled, rather than stewed, means they remain beautifully whole.

---

6 oz (175g) sugar

10 fl oz (300ml) boiling water

1 lb (450g) gooseberries, washed, topped and tailed

---

1   Make a syrup by stirring the sugar into the water until dissolved. Allow to cool a little.

2   Meanwhile put the gooseberries into a warmed 2 lb (1kg) jar which either has a clip-on rubber seal or a screw band. Pour over enough syrup to just cover the fruit.

3   Choose a large pot (a pressure cooker is ideal) and place a trivet or thick layer of newspaper in the bottom. Set the jar on this and pour in enough warm water to reach the same level as the fruit.

4   Now, leaving the jar slightly open, bring the water very slowly to simmering point. This should take between 25 and 30 minutes.

5   Then simmer for precisely 15 minutes. Do not cover the pot, so you can keep an eye on the temperature. Make sure it does not boil.

6   Then remove from the heat and tighten the lid immediately.

7   Cool for at least 12 hours before serving. Alternatively, store as a conserve, in a cool place.

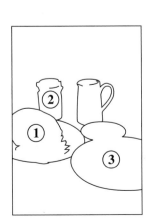

KEY
1   Clootie Dumpling – *Page 105*
2   Bottled Gooseberries – *Page 109*
3   Orkney Cheesecake with Toffee and Lemon – *Page 116*

Gooseberry and Elderflower Flan

(serves 6-8)

If you are unable to obtain elderflowers, this recipe is still good without them. If you are able to include them, you'll find the combination of flavours sublime.

For the pastry

1½ oz (35g) margarine
1½ oz (35g) lard
6 oz (175g) plain flour, sifted
pinch of salt
cold water

For the filling

1 lb 4 oz (560g) gooseberries, washed but not topped and tailed
2 fl oz (50ml) sherry
3 oz (75g) sugar
10 elderflower heads, florets removed with a fork
a little caster sugar (optional)
2 oz (50g) butter (not margarine)
3 large eggs, beaten
gooseberry leaves

Preheat oven to 200°C, 180°C for Fan oven, 400°F, Gas Mark 6

1 Rub the fats into the flour and salt until the mixture resembles fine breadcrumbs. Add enough cold water to form a smooth dough and allow to rest in a cool place for 30 minutes.

2 Then roll out the pastry to line a greased flan tin, 8-9 inches by 1½ inches deep (20-22 cm by 3 cm).

3 Prick with a fork and bake blind for 15 minutes.

4 Meanwhile, put the gooseberries, sherry and sugar into a saucepan. Cover and cook gently for 10 minutes. Then remove the lid, increase the heat and allow to reduce for 4-5 minutes, stirring continuously.

5 Next remove from the heat, stirring in the elderflowers as soon as you do so.

6 Rub the mixture through a sieve until only a dryish ball remains. Taste the purée and add a little caster sugar if desired.

7 Now put the purée into a clean pan along with the butter and beaten eggs. Stir the mixture over a gentle heat until it thickens. Do not allow to boil.

8 Pour immediately into the pastry case and chill well. Garnish with the gooseberry leaves and serve with single cream.

Redcurrant Clafoutis

(serves 8-10)

If you are unable to obtain redcurrants, you can substitute them with raspberries or sliced strawberries. Serve the clafoutis lukewarm with cream and you'll discover a slice of heaven.

For the pastry

7 oz (200g) plain flour, sifted
1 oz (25g) cornflour, sifted
5 oz (150g) butter, cut into small pieces
1 oz (25g) caster sugar
1 medium egg, lightly beaten

For the filling

3 oz (75g) sugar
3½ oz (100g packet) ground almonds
2 large eggs
5 fl oz (150ml) single cream
1 dessertspoonful melted butter
12 oz (340g) fresh redcurrants, removed from their stalks

Preheat oven to 200°C, 180°C for Fan oven, 400°F, Gas Mark 6

1 Put the flours into a bowl and rub in the butter until the mixture resembles breadcrumbs. Then stir in the sugar and egg. Chill for 20 minutes.

2 Meanwhile whisk the sugar, ground almonds, eggs and cream together in a bowl. Add the butter and continue to whisk for a few moments.

3 Now roll out the pastry on a well floured surface and use it to line 2 greased 8 inch (20 cm) flan tins. Prick with a fork.

4 Put the redcurrants in the base of the flans and pour over the ground almond mixture.

5 Bake for 25 minutes or until light golden brown.

Blackcurrant Jelly

(serves 4-5)

A home-made jelly is much superior to bought varieties. This one is so bursting
with the flavour of fruit that it is almost for adults only.

12 oz (340g) blackcurrants, washed (there is no
need to top and tail them)

8 oz (225g) sugar

4 fl oz (100ml) dry white wine

cold water

½ oz (11g sachet) powdered gelatine

1 Put the blackcurrants into a saucepan with the sugar and wine. Bring to the boil, cover and simmer for 8 minutes.

2 Place a sieve over a bowl and pour the blackcurrants into this. Allow to drip for 3 minutes without stirring.

3 Meanwhile put 2 fl oz (50ml) water into a small bowl and stir in the powdered gelatine. Set this over a saucepan of simmering water and stir until the gelatine dissolves.

4 Next discard the contents of the sieve and give it a quick rinse. Pour the dissolved gelatine through this and into the bowl of juice.

5 Stir and top up to the 1 pint (600ml) mark with cold water. Chill until set.

6 Serve with Orkney ice cream or whisky flummery.

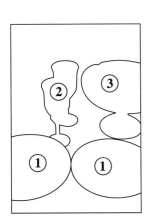

KEY
1   Redcurrant Clafoutis – *Page 111*
2   Malt Whisky Flummery – *Page 119* and Blackcurrant Jelly – *Page 113*
3   Easy Strawberry Ice Cream – *Page 118*

Terrine of Orkney Farm Cheese with Caramelised Oatmeal and Strawberry Coulis

(serves 4)

The three colours and textures of this beautiful sweet will enhance any summer dinner party. If you have raspberries, you can substitute them for the strawberries. Choose a moist, young cheese for best results.

For the terrine

8 oz (225g) Orkney farm cheese, skinned and chopped
5 fl oz (150ml) natural yoghurt
½ oz (11g sachet) powdered gelatine
5 fl oz (150ml) single cream
2 oz (50g) caster sugar
1½ tsp natural vanilla essence

For the caramelised oatmeal

1½ oz (35g) pinhead oatmeal
2 oz (50g) caster sugar
3 tbsp water

For the coulis and garnish

8 oz (225g) hulled strawberries
1 tbsp lemon juice
2-3 tsp icing sugar
8 strawberries, not hulled (to garnish)

1 Whizz the cheese with the yoghurt in a food processor or liquidiser until smooth. For perfect results, rub through a sieve.

2 Next, using a small bowl, mix the gelatine with 2 tbsp of the cream. Place the bowl in a saucepan of hot water and stir until dissolved.

3 Now pour the rest of the cream into another saucepan. Stir in the sugar and warm gently until dissolved.

4 Add the gelatine mixture and stir until evenly textured. Allow to cool a little.

5 Meanwhile, put the cheese mixture into a bowl and add the essence. Then strain the contents of the saucepan through a sieve into the bowl and whisk thoroughly.

6 Pour immediately into a 1 pint (600ml) plastic mould and chill until set (about 2-3 hours).

7 Meanwhile, make the caramelised oatmeal. Using a frying pan, toast the oatmeal over a medium heat. Stir frequently to ensure the oatmeal browns evenly. Remove to a bowl to prevent overcooking.

8 Dissolve the sugar in the water using a small saucepan over a medium heat. Increase the heat and caramelise, without stirring, until golden brown.

9 Immediately stir in the oatmeal and quickly pour the mixture onto a greased baking tray.

10 When cold, crush this using a rolling pin and plastic bags. Then crush further with a pestle and mortar.

11 To make the coulis, liquidise the strawberries with the lemon juice and icing sugar. Strain to remove the pips.

12 To assemble, remove the terrine from the mould and slice into 4 pieces, trimming the edges if necessary.

13 Place each slice on a plate and top with an even layer of caramelised oatmeal. Pour round the coulis and garnish with the strawberries.

< Terrine of Orkney Farm Cheese with Caramelised Oatmeal and Strawberry Coulis

Orkney Cheesecake with Toffee and Lemon

(serves 8)

Made from Orkney farm cheese and topped with Orkney fudge, this cheesecake sounds rich. The presence of lemon, however, gives a good balance of sharp and sweet flavours.

1 tin (218g) sweetened, condensed milk
8 oz (225g) sweet, oat biscuits, crushed
3 oz (75g) butter, melted
½ oz (11g sachet) powdered gelatine
4 tbsp cold water
2 oz (50g) caster sugar

juice and rind of one lemon
5 oz (150g) Orkney farm cheese, skinned and chopped
3 oz (75g) cottage cheese
5 fl oz (150ml) single cream
a few squares Orkney fudge, grated

1 Boil the tin of milk, unopened, in a saucepan of water for two hours. Remember to check that the water level remains high. Cool when cooked.

2 Meanwhile, mix the biscuit crumbs with the butter. Press this mixture into a 9 inch (22 cm), loose-bottomed flan tin. Chill until firm.

3 Open the tin of condensed milk, which by now will have turned to toffee, and spread this evenly over the biscuit base, to within ½ an inch (1 cm) of the edge.

4 In a small saucepan, mix the gelatine, water and sugar. Allow to stand, without warming, for 5 minutes.

5 Meanwhile put the lemon juice, lemon rind, both cheeses and the cream into a food processor. Whizz until smooth. Alternatively, rub the cheeses through a sieve, before whisking in the lemon ingredients and cream.

6 Next warm the gelatine mixture very gently, stirring constantly as you do so.

7 When the gelatine has dissolved, hold a sieve over the cheese mixture and pour the syrup through this.

8 Give a final whizz and pour quickly over the layer of toffee.

9 Chill until set. Remove from the flan tin just before serving and garnish with the grated fudge.

Orkney Bread and Butter Pudding

(serves 6-7)

Recently a loaf of bread with a subtle beremeal flavour has appeared in some Orkney shops. This product, along with local butter and some Orkney fudge, can produce a pudding with a unique character.

14 slices bere bread (from a small, thinly sliced loaf)	1 pint (600ml) milk
Orkney butter	2 oz (50g) soft brown sugar
3 eggs	1 packet (100g) Orkney fudge

Preheat oven to 180°C, 160°C for Fan oven, 350°F, Gas Mark 4

1 Begin by buttering the bread and cutting each slice into 4 small triangles.

2 Then grease a large, flat, ovenproof dish and place the bread in an overlapping layer in the bottom of this.

3 Mix the eggs, milk and sugar until evenly amalgamated and pour this all over the bread.

4 Now grate the fudge over the top and bake for about 30 minutes.

5 Serve with cream or Orkney ice cream.

Alan's Tip:

"Jelly will set more quickly if you use ice cubes when topping up to the 1 pint mark."

Easy Strawberry Ice Cream

(Makes approximately 4 pints or 2 ½ litres)

The presence of egg white in this recipe means the ice cream can be made in one
go and does not need to be removed from the freezer at various intervals
to be whisked.

1 lb (450g) strawberries (hulled weight)	6 tbsp water
10 oz (275g) caster sugar	½ pint (300ml) whipping cream
3 tbsp lemon juice	5 fl oz (150ml) natural yoghurt
3 small egg whites (or 2 large)	1½ tsp natural vanilla essence

1 First whizz the strawberries in a blender with 4 oz (110g) of the sugar and the lemon juice. Check sugar has dissolved.

2 In your largest bowl, whisk the egg whites until stiff.

3 Next, using a small saucepan, dissolve the remaining sugar in the water over a gentle heat. Increase the heat and boil for 3 minutes.

4 Now carefully pour this syrup into the egg whites in a steady trickle, whisking continuously as you do so. This will cook and thicken the egg whites. Continue to whisk for 3 minutes.

5 In another bowl, whisk the cream until stiff and stir in the yoghurt.

6 Then fold this into the egg mixture and add the vanilla essence.

7 Gently stir in the liquid strawberries. Stop mixing before the colour is uniform if you want your ice cream to have a marbled effect.

8 Freeze in a plastic container.

9 Remove to the fridge 30 minutes before serving. This will achieve a better consistency than leaving at room temperature.

Honey Ice Cream

(serves 4)

Here is a rare opportunity to make a dessert entirely from Orkney ingredients –
locally produced honey, fresh double cream, free-range eggs and lemon balm
from your garden.

---

4 egg yolks
2 level tbsp honey

10 fl oz (300ml) double cream
lemon balm (to garnish)

---

1 Put the egg yolks and honey into a bowl and set this over a saucepan of simmering water.

2 Whisk continuously until pale and thick. The mixture should leave a ribbon trail when the whisk is lifted. Allow to cool slightly.

3 Then beat the cream until stiff and stir this into the egg mixture.

4 Pour this into a plastic container and freeze until firm. There is no need to remove from the freezer to whisk at intervals as there is little water content in this ice cream.

5 Garnish with lemon balm and serve with shortbread.

Malt Whisky Flummery

(serves 4)

Serve this rich dessert with some fresh raspberries
or a home-made blackcurrant jelly.

---

4 egg yolks
4 oz (110g) caster sugar
3 tbsp malt whisky

5 fl oz (150ml) double cream
demerara sugar (to garnish)

---

1 Put the egg yolks and caster sugar into a bowl and whip over a saucepan of simmering water until pale and thick.

2 Next add the whisky and continue beating for 1-2 minutes. The mixture will be thinner now.

3 Then whip the cream until stiff and stir into the whisky mixture.

4 Serve in individual glasses with the tops sprinkled with a little demerara sugar.

Bakes

I have many childhood memories of my mother baking on the kitchen stove. I can recall rainy Saturday afternoons in the 1950s, with football results on the wireless and flour bannocks, oatcakes, drop scones and oven scones being made for tea, to be eaten, spanking fresh, with farm butter or homemade jam.

The homebaking tradition in Orkney stretches far into the past and the expertise which exists in this field should, in no way, be underrated. The bakes in this book, I hope, reflect that long tradition. Some are part of our culture, such as bere bannocks and oatcakes, while other recipes include honey, a more recent ingredient in Orkney's produce list.

Oven temperatures are nowhere so critical as in this chapter of the book. In many cases there is only a minute's leeway on either side of the cooking time for those elusive, perfect results. All those who bake know their ovens better than I ever could, so oven temperatures and cooking times in the following recipes are a rough guide only.

*A girnel stood against the wall
with meal baith ait and bere.*

Dialect Poem, M. Russell

Bere Bannocks

(makes 1)

In the old days, these were made solely from beremeal, but nowadays ordinary flour is also included. Some bakers use twice as much beremeal as flour, but I find equal quantities of each a balance which appeals to many palates.

2 oz (50g) beremeal	*pinch of salt*
2 oz (50g) self-raising flour	*1 tsp cooking oil*
1 level tsp baking soda	*approximately 2½ fl oz (60ml) water*
1 level tsp cream of tartar	

1 Sieve all the dry ingredients into a bowl. Stir in the oil and add enough water to form a dough which leaves the bowl clean. Beat well.

2 Then, on a floured surface, shape into a 6 inch (15cm) round.

3 Dust a hot girdle with flour and bake the bannock for a few minutes on each side until risen.

4 If you want a perfectly soft bannock, wrap it in kitchen roll and then a towel so that steam does not escape during the cooling process.

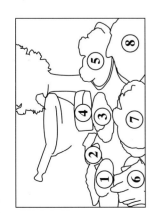

KEY
1   Bere Bannocks – *Page 123*
2   Fattie Cutties – *Page 134*
3   Flour Bannocks – *Page 124*
4   Honey and Lemon Tea Loaf – *Page 131*
5   Oven Scones – *Page 126*
6   Thin Pancakes – *Page 128*
7   Honey Oat Biscuits – *Page 130*
8   Drop Scones – *Page 125*

Flour Bannocks

(makes 3)

Souring the milk with vinegar gives these bannocks a more authentic quality. Try them freshly baked with any kind of Orkney cheese.

3 fl oz (75ml) milk, approximately	*1 level tsp cream of tartar*
1 tbsp vinegar	*good pinch of salt*
8 oz (225g) self-raising flour	*1 medium egg, beaten*
1 level tsp baking soda	*1 tbsp melted margarine*

1 Pour the milk into a bowl, add the vinegar and set aside for a few minutes.

2 Meanwhile sieve the flour, baking soda, cream of tartar and salt into a mixing bowl. Make a well in the middle and add the egg and melted margarine.

3 Gradually whisk the egg and margarine into the dry ingredients, pouring in the milk, a little at a time, when the mixture becomes stiff. Do not add all the milk if you find you have the right consistency to form into rounds.

4 Now divide the mixture into 3 and shape into 6 inch (15 cm) rounds on a floured surface.

5 Dust a medium hot girdle with flour and bake each bannock until risen and light brown on both sides.

6 As with bere bannocks, cool them between layers of kitchen roll and a towel, to preserve softness of texture.

Drop Scones

(makes about 20)

There are as many pancake recipes as there are houses in Orkney.
Here is one which, I think, works particularly well.

1 large egg	1 rounded tsp cream of tartar
2 oz (50g) caster sugar	1 level tsp baking soda
1 tsp syrup	good pinch of salt
8 oz (225g) self-raising flour	6-7 fl oz (175-200ml) milk

1   Whisk the egg, sugar and syrup together in a bowl.

2   Sift the flour into another bowl and add the cream of tartar, baking soda and salt.

3   Now make a well in the flour and pour in the beaten egg. Gradually whisk the egg to incorporate the flour, adding the milk, a little at a time, when the mixture gets stiff.

4   Once a soft dropping consistency has been achieved, grease a medium hot girdle and bake dessertspoonfuls of the mixture, a few at a time.

5   Turn before the bubbles burst and cool on a towel.

Alan's Tip:

"Cut a lemon into slices and freeze them near your ice

cubes in readiness for drinks."

Oven Scones

(makes 8)

These are the best oven scones I have tasted. They freeze well and, if thawed in the microwave, are as fresh as the minute they were baked.

3 oz (75g) self-raising flour	2 oz (50g) margarine
3 oz (75g) plain flour	1 medium egg
2 rounded tsp baking powder	1 fl oz (25ml) milk
1 oz sugar	

Preheat oven to 210°C, 190°C for Fan oven, 425°F, Gas Mark 7

1 Sift the flours and baking powder into a bowl and add the sugar. Then rub in the margarine until the mixture resembles fine breadcrumbs.

2 Make a well in the middle and break the egg into this. Add the milk and mix to form a dough.

3 Now roll out the dough on a floured surface until ½ inch (1 cm) thick. Cut into rounds with a 2½ inch (6 cm) cutter.

4 Bake the scones for 9-12 minutes on a floured baking sheet. Cool on a wire tray.

Tattie Scones

(makes 16)

These are good with bacon and eggs for breakfast, but it is probably more common in Orkney to eat them at tea-time with cheese or a fry up.

8 oz (225g) mashed potato	salt and pepper
2 oz (50g) plain flour	splash of milk

1 Mix the potato, flour and seasoning in a bowl, adding enough milk to bind to a dough.

2 Divide the mixture in two and, using plenty of flour, roll these into 9 inch (22 cm) rounds.

3 Cut each into 8 pieces and bake these on a greased, medium hot girdle until lightly browned on both sides.

4 Spread with butter and serve while still warm.

Treacle Oven Scones

(makes 10-12)

These are delicious with butter, but if you are into sweet and savoury tastes together, try them with some cream cheese.

8 oz (225g) self-raising flour	2 fl oz (50ml) milk
pinch of salt	2 tbsp treacle
2¹/₂ oz (60g) butter, cut into pieces	1 oz (25g) soft brown sugar
1 medium egg, lightly beaten	1 level tsp mixed spice

Preheat oven to 220°C, 200°C for Fan oven, 425°F, Gas Mark 7

1 Sift the flour into a bowl and add the salt. Rub in the butter until the mixture resembles fine breadcrumbs.

2 In a separate bowl, mix all the other ingredients until the treacle is well amalgamated. Pour this into the flour and beat to remove lumps.

3 Using a generous amount of flour to prevent sticking, roll out the mixture to ¹/₂ inch (1 cm) thickness.

4 Now cut out rounds with a 2 inch (5 cm) pastry cutter and place these on a greased and floured baking tray. You will need to re-roll the dough to use it all up.

5 Bake for 12-15 minutes. The scones are ready if they sound hollow when tapped on the bottom.

6 Cool on a wire tray.

Thin Pancakes

(makes approximately 30)

This is an almost foolproof recipe, which will give you light, golden pancakes.

---

4 oz (110g) self-raising flour

4 oz (110g) plain flour

1 level tsp baking soda

1 rounded tsp cream of tartar

pinch of salt

2 oz (50g) caster sugar

1 large egg, beaten

15 fl oz (450ml) milk

---

1 Sift the flours, baking soda, cream of tartar and salt into a bowl. Stir in the sugar.

2 Then gradually whisk in the beaten egg and milk to create a consistency like single cream.

3 When all the egg and milk has been added, give the batter a final whisk and allow it to stand for a few minutes.

4 Meanwhile preheat a girdle or frying pan to a medium heat. Grease lightly.

5 Next spread tablespoonfuls of the mixture on the girdle, turning the pancakes when the bubbles have burst.

6 Cool and roll up before serving.

Oatcakes

(makes 12)

Oatcakes were originally made using kirned milk or cheese whey but, since these are now difficult to come by, I've given the equivalent amount of water.

6 oz (175g) fine oatmeal	1/2 oz (12g) margarine
1 level tsp salt	approximately 2-3 fl oz (50-75ml) hot water
1 level tsp baking soda	

1 Put the oatmeal, salt and baking soda into a bowl. Then rub in the margarine.

2 For best results divide the mixture in two and splash half the hot water into one batch only. This will make the oatcakes easier to roll out.

3 Once you have made a dough, roll it out into an 8 inch (20 cm) round, dusting under and over with oatmeal to prevent sticking.

4 Now cut the round into 6 pieces and cook these on a hot girdle or heavy frying pan until the edges just curl.

5 While the first oatcake is cooking, you can add the water to the second batch of oatmeal and roll it out.

6 Finish the upper sides of the oatcakes by transferring to a hot grill, being careful not to let them brown.

Alan's Tip:

"Always remove cheese from the fridge and unwrap it

at least an hour before you intend to eat it.

The flavour is much better after the cheese has breathed

at room temperature."

Honey Oat Biscuits

(makes 22, approximately)

We use Orkney honey when we make these in our house. The results are invariably delicious.

3 oz (75g) porage oats	4 oz (110g) margarine
4 oz (110g) plain flour, sifted	1 tbsp honey
3 oz (75g) sugar	1 tsp baking soda
1 tsp baking powder	

Preheat oven to 200°C, 180°C for Fan oven, 400°F, Gas Mark 6

1   Begin by mixing the porage oats, flour, sugar and baking powder in a bowl.

2   In a saucepan, stir the remaining three ingredients over a gentle heat until the margarine is melted. Then pour these into the bowl and mix well.

3   Now, using teaspoonfuls of the mixture, roll into balls and flatten.

4   Place these on greased and lined baking trays, spacing them out well to allow for expansion in the oven.

5   Bake for 9-10 minutes. Cool slightly before removing from baking trays.

Honey and Lemon Tea Loaf

(for a 2 lb or 1kg sized loaf)

This is my wife's recipe for a tea loaf that is delicately textured and not too sweet.

1 oz (25g) margarine	1 level tsp baking powder
6 tbsp Orkney honey	4 tbsp milk
1 egg	2 tbsp lemon juice
6 oz (175g) self-raising flour, sifted	grated rind of 1 lemon
1 pinch salt	

Preheat oven to 180°C, 160°C for Fan oven, 350°F, Gas Mark 4

1 Cream the margarine with the honey in a bowl. Then beat in the egg.

2 Gradually add the flour, salt and baking powder along with the milk, beating well between each addition.

3 Then mix in the lemon juice and rind.

4 Pour the mixture into a greased, lined 2 lb (1kg) loaf tin and bake for 45-55 minutes or until cooked.

5 Remove from the tin and peel off the paper. Allow to cool before slicing.

Alan's Tip:

"To make perfect breadcrumbs, lightly grill them before

giving a final whizz in the food processor."

Shortbread

(makes 16 triangles)

Considering the simplicity of ingredients, it is amazing how many approaches there are to making shortbread. The method below involves creaming the butter and will give you melt-in-the-mouth results.

3 oz (75g) slightly salted butter	*6 oz (175g) plain flour, sifted*
1 oz (25g) block margarine	*extra caster sugar, for dredging*
2 oz caster sugar	

Preheat oven to 170°C, 150°C for Fan oven, 325°F, Gas Mark 3

1 Cream the butter and margarine together. Then beat in the sugar.

2 Next stir in the flour until evenly amalgamated.

3 Knead lightly on a floured surface until smooth. Do not do this for too long or the butter will melt with the heat of your hand.

4 Now divide the mixture in two and roll out each into a 6 inch (15 cm) round. Mark the edges with a fork and, using a large knife, cut each into 8 segments. Prick with a fork.

5 Place these side by side on a greased baking sheet and bake for about 25 minutes in the centre of the oven. The shortbread is ready when it is a light straw colour.

6 Remove the tray from the oven and dredge the shortbread with caster sugar. Cool on a wire tray.

Rhubarb Jam Tart

(makes 2)

If you have excess jars of rhubarb jam in your cupboard, this is a good way of using them up. You might also like to experiment with other jams, which are equally well suited to the recipe.

6 oz (175g) butter	8 oz (225g) plain flour, sifted
3 oz (75g) sugar	1 tsp baking powder
1 egg	4 tbsp home-made rhubarb jam

Preheat oven to 190°C, 170°C for Fan oven, 375°F, Gas Mark 5

1 Grease and line 2 x 7 inch (17 cm) sandwich tins.

2 Beat the butter and sugar together until creamy. Then beat in the egg, flour and baking powder to form a dough.

3 Divide the dough in 2 equal pieces. Roll out just over half of each piece and line the base of each tin, pushing the dough a little way up the sides. You will find the dough quite soft to work with. Do not feel you have to be too tidy as you would with pastry.

4 Next spread 2 tablespoons of jam over each base and fold the dough from the sides of the tins.

5 Roll out the remaining dough to make 2 x 7 inch (17 cm) circles. Place these on top of the jam, pressing down the edges.

6 Bake for 30 minutes or until golden. Allow to cool in the tins before removing paper and slicing into wedges.

Alan's Tip:

"Try placing fresh or dried mint in the bottom of hot chocolate for an unusual taste."

Fattie Cutties

(makes 8)

Try these when they're freshly made and spread with butter or home-made jam.

5 oz (150g) plain flour	*2 oz (50g) currants*
pinch of salt	*3 oz (75g) margarine*
½ level tsp baking soda	*1 fl oz (25ml) milk*
1½ oz (35g) sugar	

1 Sift the flour, salt and baking soda into a bowl. Stir in the sugar and currants.

2 Then melt the margarine and add this to the mixture. Pour in the milk and combine all the ingredients to form a dough.

3 Now divide the mixture into two and roll each half on a floured surface to form a 6 inch (15 cm) square. Cut each into 4 smaller squares.

4 Cook the fattie cutties on a medium hot girdle which has been dusted with a little flour.

5 Turn once, when golden, and cool on a wire tray.

Black Bun

It is worthwhile making a large black bun as it not only keeps well, but also improves with age.
To adhere to tradition, serve this on Hogmanay.

For the pastry

12 oz (340g) plain flour
pinch of salt
4 oz (110g) hard margarine, cut into pieces
cold water
1 small egg, beaten

For the filling

2 lb (900g) currants
2 lb (900g) raisins
8 oz (225g) ground almonds
4 oz (110g) mixed peel
½ oz (12g) dried ginger
½ oz (12g) cinnamon
½ oz (12g) allspice
good grating of black pepper
8 oz (225g) sugar
1 lb (450g) plain flour
1 level tsp baking soda
1 level tsp cream of tartar
up to 10 fl oz (300ml) milk
1 egg, beaten

Preheat oven to 180°C, 160°C for Fan oven, 350°F, Gas Mark 4

1 To make the pastry, sift the flour and salt into a bowl and rub in the margarine until the mixture resembles breadcrumbs. Add just enough water to form a dough and allow to rest in a cool place for 30 minutes.

2 Meanwhile mix the fruit, almonds, peel, spices and sugar together in a roomy bowl. Sift the flour and add to the fruit.

3 Now dissolve the soda and cream of tartar in half of the milk. Add this to the fruit mixture along with the beaten egg.

4 Mix thoroughly, adding more milk until you have a dropping consistency.

5 Next grease a 9½ inch (24 cm) round cake tin.

6 Reserving some pastry for the top of the bun, roll out the rest on a floured surface and line the bottom and sides of the tin in one piece. The pastry should be rolled very thinly (⅛ inch or 3 mm) and should overhang the tin slightly. Put filling into pastry shell.

7 After that, roll out the remaining pastry to form a lid. Turn in the overhanging edges, dampen slightly and fit the lid on top, sealing well.

8 Prick all over with a fork and make 4 holes right down to the bottom using a skewer.

9 Brush the top with beaten egg.

10 Bake for 3-4 hours. Check after 3 hours and if a skewer comes out clean when inserted into the bun, then remove from the oven. If you have a fan oven, check before three hours.

Drinks

Orkney has, for better and for worse, a long history of brewing and merrymaking. In olden days, home brewed ales were made 'straight from the bere' in wooden fermenting barrels, which frothed beside peat fires. Nowadays brewing kits and sophisticated equipment have largely replaced old-fashioned methods. As a compromise between old and new, the home brew recipe in this book uses extract of malt and dried hops.

The Orkney Brewery in the West Mainland produces some high calibre beers with diverse characteristics. As well as being most satisfying drinks in their own right, some of the more full-bodied ales lend themselves to cookery, particularly carbonnades.

Country wines are made by some enthusiasts from a host of ingredients — potatoes, carrots, rhubarb, gooseberries, dandelions and primroses — to name but a few. Still other ingredients offer themselves to a selection of soft drinks.

Orkney boasts Scotland's two most northerly distilleries, Highland Park and Scapa — gems indeed for connoisseurs of malt whisky. Sitting by a roaring fire with friends, while a winter gale howls outside, and sipping those amber drops, themselves the essence of summers long past, is one of the great delights of living in this unique part of the world.

*The scattered yeast grains coalesce,
the mass heaves and multiplies, the
whole kirn is possessed by a gentle
seething, sighing, whispering.
The brew begins to sing.*

Letters from Hamnavoe, George Mackay Brown

Home Brew

(makes 5 gallons or 23 litres)

This recipe from the island of Westray produces a medium strength beer that
you'll find incredibly moreish.

2½ oz (60g) lager type hops
1 tin (1½kg) light extract of malt
3½ lb (1½kg) sugar

1 sachet brewing yeast
extra sugar for bottling

---

1 Put the hops into a muslin bag and boil them for 30 minutes in plenty of water in your largest pot. Pour the liquid into a sterilised brewing bin.

2 To extract maximum flavour, repeat this process using fresh water. Then squeeze the hops dry and discard them, reserving all liquid in the bin.

3 Next dissolve the extract of malt and sugar in the hot liquid and top up to the 5 gallon (23 litre) mark with cold water (and perhaps some hot) until the temperature is lukewarm.

4 Sprinkle over the yeast, cover loosely and leave to ferment in a warm place for 6-9 days.

5 As soon as fermentation is over, siphon into sterilised bottles, being careful not to disturb the sediment at the bottom of the bin. Leave 1½ inches (3½ cm) space between the top and the beer. Add one level teaspoon of sugar to each bottle.

6 Cork the bottles tightly and leave to stand in a warm place for 3 days. Then remove to a cool place until clear.

7 The brew is ready to drink after 7 days but will improve with age.

KEY
1   Home Brew – *Page 139*
2   Mulled Home Brew – *Page 140*
3   Tattie Wine – *Page 142*

Mulled Home Brew

(Makes enough for 8-9 mugs)

Serve this most reassuring drink, steaming hot, around Christmas. Use brown ale
if you don't brew yourself.

1 satsuma, studded with 8 cloves	½ level tsp ground nutmeg
2 pints (1 litre 200ml) home brew (not lager)	2 pinches ground ginger
15 fl oz (450ml) apple juice	4 fl oz (100ml) sherry
6 tbsp muscovado sugar	½ large lemon, sliced

1 Bake the satsuma for 15 minutes in a moderate oven.

2 Put all the ingredients into a large saucepan. Bring to near simmering point, stirring occasionally to help the sugar dissolve.

3 Remove from the heat and serve, piping hot, in mugs or heated glasses.

Orkney Nightcap

(serves 1)

Unlike oatmeal based nightcaps, which take some time to make, this one can be made
in seconds. Sip it slowly just before bedtime and you'll immediately start to unwind.

8 fl oz (225ml) milk	1½ tbsp Orkney whisky
1 tsp Orkney honey	1 heaped tsp malted milk drink

1 Put the milk and honey into a saucepan and bring slowly to simmering point.

2 Meanwhile, stir the whisky and malted milk drink together in a mug.

3 When the milk is ready, pour into the mug, stirring until mixed.

Meadowsweet Cup

(serves 5-6)

Meadowsweet blossoms are plentiful in Orkney over the summer months. Here
they are used to perfume some red wine in a delightful aperitif.

3 meadowsweet heads	1 bottle red wine (Bordeaux is suitable)

1 Shake the flowers to remove any insects and leave them to infuse in the wine for about 2 hours.

2 Strain before serving in wine glasses.

Bride's Cog

(for 2 cogs)

Traditionally this is made from home brew but brown ale is a good substitute if you don't brew yourself. This recipe calls for a bottle of whisky minus one nip. Perhaps the cog maker can work out what to do with the missing dram.

5 bottles home brew	¼ bottle dark rum
1-1½ lb (450-675g) demerara sugar, approximately	½ bottle port
1 bottle whisky, minus one nip	mixed spice (optional)

1 Pour the home brew into a large pot, being careful not to disturb any sediment at the bottom of the bottles.

2 Add three quarters of the sugar and heat the mixture, stirring from time to time.

3 When almost boiling, add the whisky, rum and port.

4 Now apply a gentle heat to raise the temperature slightly. Do **not** allow to boil, otherwise you will seriously impair the alcohol content (and consequently the wedding).

5 Now get someone of the opposite sex to taste the cog with you, adding more sugar and the spice (if used) until you both agree the cog is perfect. If you are unsure, it is usually best to err on the sweet side.

6 Call the bride and groom, and be the first to toast them with the cog.

Strawberry and Honey Milk Shake

(serves 2)

Overlooked to some extent, milk shakes provide us with some easy and varied substitutes for puddings. This is one of the best I've tasted.

16 fl oz (475ml) full cream milk, chilled	½ tsp natural vanilla essence
8 oz (225g) strawberries, hulled	4 tsp honey
1 scoop Orkney vanilla ice cream	

1 Whizz all the ingredients together in a food processor or liquidiser until smooth.

2 Then strain to remove the pips and serve immediately in tall glasses.

Orkney Fudge and Banana Milk Shake

(serves 2)

Despite its sweetness, this offers good nutritional value. Into the bargain, kids will love it.

16 fl oz (475ml) full cream milk, chilled	1 banana, peeled
6 squares Orkney fudge	1 scoop Orkney vanilla ice cream

1 Pour a little of the milk into your food processor or liquidiser. Then add the fudge and whizz on full power. You may find you still have small pieces of fudge in the milk but children will love these.

2 Next blend in the rest of the milk, the banana and the ice cream.

3 Serve immediately in tall glasses.

Tattie Wine

(makes 2 gallons or 9 litres)

Strong, dry tattie wine makes every bit as good an aperitif as a sherry or a gin martini. This recipe comes originally from the island of Papa Westray.

4 lb (1kg 800g) demerara sugar	2 lb (900g) raisins
1 lb (450g) honey	4 lb (1kg 800g) old potatoes, scrubbed
2 oranges	(not peeled) and diced
1 lemon	1 oz (25g) dried wine yeast
1 lime	

1 Dissolve the sugar and honey in 4 pints (2 litres 400ml) boiling water.

2 Grate the zest from the citrus fruit and chop the flesh (and pith) into small pieces. Add the zest, fruit and any escaped juices to the dissolved sugar and stir in the raisins. Allow to cool slightly.

3 Meanwhile, divide the potatoes between two sterilised demijohns. Then pour in the sugar and fruit mixture equally over the potatoes.

4 Add enough cold water to come to 2 inches (5cm) below the top of the demijohns and, when the liquid is lukewarm, sprinkle half the yeast into each jar.

5 Put fermenting locks on the demijohns and leave in a warm place until the bubbles stop.

6 Then strain and bottle the wine in sterilised bottles. Cork and leave in a cool place for at least 2 months. The wine will improve with age.

Rhubarb Wine

(for 2½ gallons or 11½ litres)

This recipe produces a very pleasant drink, which can either be sipped by itself or topped up with mineral water.

12½ lb (5½ kg) young, red rhubarb, topped and tailed	1¼ lb (560g) sultanas
Milton sterilising solution	1 gallon (4½ litres) boiling water
thinly peeled rind of 2 oranges	2 oz (50g) precipitated chalk
thinly peeled rind of 1 lemon	6-7 lbs (2kg 700g-3kg 150g) sugar
	1 sachet high speed wine yeast

1 Put the rhubarb into a large container with enough cold water to cover and the correct amount of sterilising solution for food. (See bottle for details). Leave for 30 minutes.

2 Meanwhile, put the orange and lemon rind into a saucepan. Cover with water, put on a lid and boil for 2 minutes.

3 Now rinse the rhubarb thoroughly and cut into 1 inch (2 cm) lengths. Put these into a sterilised fermenting bin along with the orange peel, lemon peel (plus the liquid) and the sultanas.

4 Pour over the boiling water, cover tightly and leave to stand for 5-7 days in a cool, dark place.

5 After that, discard all the fruit and stir the precipitated chalk into the liquid.

6 In a large saucepan, dissolve the sugar in approximately 3 pints (1¾ litres) boiling water and stir this into the fermenting bin. Top up to the 2½ gallon (11½ litre) mark with cold water. Test that the liquid is no hotter than lukewarm and sprinkle over the yeast.

7 Transfer to 1 large or 3 small demijohns with air locks and leave in a warm place for about 6 weeks. Allow plenty of space between the wine and the tops of the jars because of fermentation.

8 When the bubbles cease to appear in the air locks, move to a cooler place for several more weeks.

9 For best results, siphon the wine into clean jars and allow to become quite clear before bottling. Be careful not to disturb any sediment in the siphoning process.

10 As with other wines, this will improve with age.

Index

Arctic Char with Smitaine Sauce 41

Baked Field Mushrooms 65
Baked Haddock with Cous Cous and Roast Vegetable Stuffing 34
Baked Onions 71
Baked Parsnips with Orkney Cheese 74
Baked Potatoes with Watercress and Cottage Cheese 63
Bannocks
       Bere 123
       Flour 124
Barley, Herbed 93
Beef
       Beef and Oyster Pie 81
       Beef in Dark Island Ale with Oatmeal and Mustard Doughboys 82
       Beef Olives 90
       Curried Beef Sausages 89
       Salted, Spiced Brisket 83
       Savoury Mince with Root Vegetable Topping 85
       Sirloin Steak with Whisky and Ginger Sauce 84
       Spiced Beefburgers 89
       Steamed Mince Pudding 87
       Stuffed Meatballs in Tomato Sauce 88
Beetroot
       Beetroot with Lime 75
       Soup 19
Bere Bannocks 123
Black Bun 135
Blackcurrant Jelly 113
Bottled Gooseberries 109
Bread and Butter Pudding 117
Bride's Cog 141
Broad Beans with Brown Lentils and Black Butter 69
Broccoli and Lemon Soup 17
Brussels Sprouts, Glazed 42

Cabbage
       Green Cabbage with Vinegar 68
       Kale and Pork and Tatties 97
       Red Cabbage, Braised with Rum, Pears and Allspice .69
       White Cabbage with Gin and Juniper Berries 68
Carrots with Cider and Rosemary 75
Cauliflower with Two Orkney Cheeses and Shallots 77
Celery with Cashew Nuts 76
Cheese
       Fried Orkney Cheese with Rhubarb Vinaigrette and Soured Cream 25
       Greek Salad, Orkney Style 70
       Grilled Cheese Omelette 52
       Marinated Goat's Cheese 53
       Orcadian Rarebit 52
       Orkney Cheesecake with Toffee and Lemon 116
       Pancakes Stuffed with Orkney Cheddar, Bacon and Apples 55
       Terrine of Orkney Farm Cheese with Caramelised Oatmeal and Strawberry Coulis .115
Chicken
       County Show Night Chicken 99
       Mock Cockie Chicken 100

Clapshot 61
Clapshot Croquettes 62
Clootie Dumpling 105
Cockles 44
Cockles in White Wine 45
Cod
     Cod in Filo Pastry with Tarragon Cream Sauce 36
     Cod Steaks with Leeks and Mushrooms 37
Consommé of Swede with Highland Park Whisky and Fresh Sage 16
Crab
     Partan and Avocado Mousse 46
Cream of Mussel Soup 18
Cuithes 32
Curried Beef Sausages 89

Deep Fried Potato Peelings 56
Deep Fried Scallops in Quick Marie Rose Sauce 19
Drop Scones 125
Duck Stir Fry 101

Easy Garden Turnip Soup 15
Easy Strawberry Ice Cream 118
Eggs
     Egg and Tomato Bake 54
     Grilled Cheese Omelette 52
     Kipper and Almond Soufflé 57
     Mayonnaise Dips 56
     Scrambled Egg on Toast, '50s Style 51

Fattie Cutties 134
Fillet of Brown Trout with Chive Butter Sauce 31
Fish Pie 32
Flour Bannocks 124
Fried Orkney Cheese with Rhubarb Vinaigrette and Soured Cream 25

Garden Turnips
     Easy Garden Turnip Soup 15
     Garden Turnip Gratin with Coriander and Lemon .65
     Garden Turnips with Oatmeal Stuffing 67
Glazed Baby Vegetables in Orkney Butter 73
Glazed Brussels Sprouts 42
Gooseberries
     Bottled Booseberries 109
     Gooseberry and Elderflower Flan 110
Greek Salad, Orkney Style 70
Green Cabbage with Vinegar 68
Grilled Cheese Omelette 52
Grilled Oysters 27

Haddock
     Baked Haddock with Cous Cous and Roast Vegetable Stuffing 34
     Marinated Fried Haddock 21
     Salt Haddock with Tatties and Melted Orkney Butter 33
     Smoked Haddock Pasty with Lemon and Caper Sauce 35

Haggis Cannelloni with a Spicy Tomato Sauce 26
Halibut Steaks with Piquant Paprika Butter 43
Herring
      Herring with Fried Apple and Glazed Brussels Sprouts .42
      Sweet Cured Herring with Pasta and Grapes 20
Highland Lobster 47
Home Brew 139
Honey
      Honey and Lemon Tea Loaf 131
      Honey Ice Cream 119
      Honey Oat Biscuits 130

Ice Cream
      Easy Strawberry Ice Cream 118
      Honey Ice Cream 119

Kale and Pork and Tatties 97
Kipper and Almond Souffle 57

Lamb
      Lamb Chops with Mint Sauce and Almonds 92
      Lamb's Liver with Herbed Barley 93
      Minced Lamb and Peanut Kebabs 92
      Summer Lamb Casserole 91
Leeks, Spiced 76
Leftovers
      Stovies 101
Lettuce and Strawberry Salad 71
Liver, Lamb's, with Herbed Barley 93
Lobster, Highland 47
Luxury Rhubarb and Apple Crumble 107

Mackerel 42
Malt Whisky Flummery 119
Mange Tout in Hot Onion Vinaigrette 70
Marinated Fried Haddock 21
Marinated Goat's Cheese 53
Mayonnaise Dips with Deep Fried Potato Peelings 56
Meadowsweet Cup 140
Meatballs, Stuffed, in Tomato Sauce 88
Milkshakes
      Orkney Fudge and Banana Milk Shake 142
      Strawberry and Honey Milk Shake 141
Minced Lamb and Peanut Kebabs 92
Mock Cockie Chicken 100
Monkfish 37
Mulled Home Brew 140
Mushrooms, Baked Field 65
Mussel Soup, Cream of 18

New Potato Bake 63
New Potatoes Paprika 64
Nightcap, Orkney 140

Oatcakes 129

Oatmeal and Mustard Doughboys 82

Omelette, Grilled Cheese 52

Onions

    Baked Onions 71

    Hot Onion Vinaigrette 70

    Onion Flan 72

    Pickled Red Onion Rings 73

Orcadian Rarebit 52

Orkney Bread and Butter Pudding 117

Orkney Cheesecake with Toffee and Lemon 116

Orkney Fudge and Banana Milk Shake 142

Orkney Nightcap 140

Oven Scones 126

Oysters

    Beef and Oyster Pie 81

    Grilled Oysters 27

Pancakes

    Pancakes Stuffed with Orkney Cheddar, Bacon and Apples 55

    Thin Pancakes 128

Parsnips, Baked with Orkney Cheese 74

Partan and Avocado Mousse 46

Pea and Potato Soup 17

Pickled Red Onion Rings 73

Plaice Fillets Stuffed with Rice and Elderflowers 39

Pork

    Kale and Pork and Tatties 97

    Pork and Apricot Meat Loaf 95

    Pork Stew with Prunes and Apples 96

    Sweet and Sour Pork Sausages 96

Potatoes

    Baked with Watercress and Cottage Cheese 63

    Clapshot 61

    Clapshot Croquettes 62

    Deep Fried Potato Peelings 56

    Kale and Pork and Tatties 97

    New Potato Bake 63

    New Potatoes Paprika 64

    Pea and Potato Soup 17

    Salad in a Mild Mustard Dressing 64

    Tattie Scones 126

    Tattie Soup 15

    Tattie Wine 142

Rarebit, Orcadian 52

Razor Fish 45

Red Cabbage, Braised with Rum, Pears and Allspice 69

Red Onion, Pickled Rings 73

Redcurrant Clafoutis 111

Rhubarb

    Luxury Rhubarb and Apple Crumble 107

    Rhubarb Fruit Sponge 106

    Rhubarb Jam Tart 133

    Rhubarb Vinaigrette 25

    Rhubarb Wine 143

Saithe 32
Salads
    Greek Salad, Orkney Style 70
    Lettuce and Strawberry Salad 71
    Potato Salad in a Mild Mustard Dressing 64
Salmon
    Salmon Fishcakes with Madeira and Mushrooms 24
    Salmon Mousse with Ginger and Orange 23
    Salmon Steaks with Yoghurt Sauce 40
    Smoked Salmon Parcels 40
Salt Haddock with Tatties and Melted Orkney Butter 33
Salted, Spiced Brisket of Beef 83
Sauces
    Chive Butter Sauce 31
    Lemon and Caper Sauce 35
    Mint Sauce and Almonds 92
    Orange and Marjoram Sauce 37
    Quick Marie Rose Sauce 19
    Smitaine Sauce 41
    Spicy Tomato Sauce 26
    Strawberry Coulis 115
    Sweet and Sour Sauce 96
    Tarragon Cream Sauce 36
    Tomato Sauce 88
    Whisky and Ginger Sauce 84
    Yoghurt Sauce 40
Sausages
    Curried Beef Sausages 89
    Sweet and Sour Pork Sausages 96
Scones
    Drop Scones 125
    Oven Scones 126
    Tattie Scones 126
    Treacle Oven Scones 127
Scrambled Egg on Toast, '50s Style 51
Sea Trout 40
Shortbread 132
Sirloin Steak with Whisky and Ginger Sauce 84
Smoked Haddock Pasty with Lemon and Caper Sauce 35
Smoked Salmon Parcels 40
Sole with Orange and Marjoram Sauce 37
Soups
    Beetroot Soup 19
    Broccoli and Lemon Soup 17
    Consommé of Swede with Highland Park Whisky and Fresh Sage ..16
    Cream of Mussel Soup 18
    Easy Garden Turnip Soup 15
    Pea and Potato Soup 17
    Tattie Soup 15
Spiced Beefburgers 89
Spiced Leeks 76
Spoots 45
Steak, Sirloin with Whisky and Ginger Sauce 84
Steamed Mince Pudding 87
Stovies 101

Index Continued

Strawberries

    Easy Strawberry Ice Cream 118

    Lettuce and Strawberry Salad 71

    Strawberry and Honey Milk Shake 141

    Strawberry Coulis 115

Stuffed Baked Tomatoes 27

Stuffed Meatballs in Tomato Sauce 88

Summer Lamb Casserole 91

Swede

    Clapshot 61

    Clapshot Croquettes 62

    Consommé of Swede with Highland Park Whisky and Fresh Sage 16

Sweet and Sour Pork Sausages 96

Sweet Cured Herring with Pasta and Grapes 20

Tattie Scones 126

Tattie Soup 15

Tattie Wine 142

Terrine of Orkney Farm Cheese with Caramelised Oatmeal and Strawberry Coulis 115

Thin Pancakes 128

Tomatoes

    Egg and Tomato Bake 54

    Greek Salad, Orkney Style 70

    Stuffed Baked Tomatoes 27

Treacle Oven Scones 127

Trout

    Brown Trout with Chive Butter Sauce 31

    Sea Trout 40

Turbot with Prawns and Mushrooms 44

Turnip

    Easy Garden Turnip Soup 15

    Garden Turnip Gratin with Coriander and Lemon 65

    Garden Turnips with Oatmeal Stuffing 67

    – see also 'Swede'

Vegetables, Glazed Baby, in Orkney Butter 73

White Cabbage with Gin and Juniper Berries 68

Wine

    Rhubarb Wine 143

    Tattie Wine 142